BY THE SAME AUTHOR

Poetry

Reading Geographies

Road Into Autumn

A Change of Season

Matelot

A Hidden Language

Criticism

The Poetry of Robert Graves

W.H. Davies: Man and Poet

The Poetry of Harold Monro

Housman's Name and Nature of Poetry

THE FORGOTTEN POET

THE FORGOTTEN POET

THE POETRY OF
EDWIN ARLINGTON ROBINSON

MICHAEL CULLUP

Greenwich Exchange
London

Greenwich Exchange, London

First published in Great Britain in 2022
All rights reserved

The Forgotten Poet: The Poetry of Edwin Arlington Robinson
© Michael Cullup, 2022

Printed and bound by imprintdigital.com
Cover design by December Publications
Tel: 07951511275

Greenwich Exchange Website: www.greenex.co.uk

Cataloguing in Publication Data is available
from the British Library

Cover:Portrait of Edwin Arlington Robinson by Lilla Carbot Perry (1916)
(courtesy of Special Collections & Archives, Colby College Libraries,
Waterville, Maine)

ISBN: 978-1-910996-60-7

CONTENTS

INTRODUCTION

I first came across a poem by Robinson so many years ago that I can no longer remember when it was, nor the anthology in which it appeared. I was immediately captured and my appetite for Robinson's poetry was revived on the very rare occasions when I came across one of his poems. And then, very recently, I was able to get hold of the 1937 *Collected Poems*. Anyone happening to come across this rare collection might well be reluctant to face up to something like 1,500 pages of apparently long or longish poems, but my own appetite remains insatiable. Some might argue that Robinson is best forgotten, especially when long poems are no longer fashionable and mainly read by students and academics. And hasn't the way poems are written changed dramatically in the past hundred years or so?

All this is true, of course, but anyone else who has had the fortune to come across an anthologised poem by Robinson (and these are almost as rare as hen's teeth) will have experienced something rather special, as I did. This experience is rare because Robinson was American and most poetry anthologies published in the United Kingodom before the advent of T.S.Eliot and Ezra Pound were devoted to British poets, and this preference has continued. It seems particularly unjust that Robinson only had two very brief mentions in the volume on American Literature which was part of the *New Pelican Guide to English Literature* (Vol 9) published in 1988 and reprinted in 1991, and with an illustrious list of contributors. Robinson is not mentioned in the reference list of 'Authors and Works' at the back of that book. This is a literary reference book that was used by most educational establishments in Britain, including the major universities. The list of contributors is an academically distinguished one, and it seems incredible that none of those contributors appears to have recognised Robinson's worth as a poet.

There is a natural inclination for particular cultures to be inward-looking, in spite of a modern tendency to claim the opposite. This is particularly the case with poetry, since the art is dependent on the nature of particular languages; hence Robert Frost's dictum that poetry is what gets lost in translation. However, poetry written in English has the advantage of reaching an audience probably larger than poetry in any other language. So the fact that American poetry, Australian poetry, Canadian poetry and the poetry of New Zealand is little read in Great Britain must be due to other factors than the language. However, within the British Isles itself, the poetry of Wales, Scotland, and Ireland is cherished, Sometimes, perhaps, more than is warranted.

My own interest in Robinson was supported by Martin Seymour-Smith's enthusiasm, and what he says about Robinson in his *A Guide to Modern World Literature* is a good starting point. Unfortunately, after that there is nowhere to go. Robinson is more or less a complete absentee on the British literary stage, and almost all of the books I have on Robinson, as well as selections from his work, were obtained from the United States.

I simply cannot understand why Robinson has been ignored here, any more than I can understand the eclipse of his popularity in the United States. He appears to be a victim of the vagaries of literary fashion, as are other particular poetic reputations. But there can be no doubt whatsoever that Robinson is a significant poet, and the eminent American literary critic Yvor Winters argued that he was a better poet than Robert Frost. This might strike the educated reader as extraordinary, but only because of Frost's established reputation as a 'major', if not 'great', poet. But Winters' views are always closely argued, with very specific textual references, and cannot be ignored. The fact that he challenged established reputations resulted in his becoming something of a maverick in the literary world, but that should have made his views more interesting, not less. It so happens that Winters wrote a very good book on Robinson: probably the best one that exists. I have listed it in the Bibliography, together with other essential references, because it is indispensable, and I shall make references to it in what follows.

Individual literary reputations are commonly sacrificed to fashion, and reputations that survive become a matter of custom and convention. Robinson has been sacrificed to this merciless process: he is the forgotten poet, almost totally absent from current views of literary history. But whether he is 'minor' or 'major' should not be the subject of debate. Robinson is a marvellous poet and I am in no doubt that he needs to be made available to a British readership.

Anyone who has never read any Robinson before will, I think, be astonished. I have tried to select poems which will have an immediate appeal (not a difficult task). Some readers will, no doubt, want to find more, but the *Collected Poems* is now long out of print. I have included what is more readily available in my Bibliography, but this is lean fare really. And it is all American. Even a *Selected Poems*, published in the Penguin Twentieth Century Classics series, emanates from the United States, is almost twenty-five years old, and is currently out of print.

The material which follows is an attempt to provide some sort of background to the poems, including a biography and a history of American attitudes to the poet, as well as other reflections on the nature of poetry and its reception. Readers who have little patience with such matters, can go directly to the fifty poems which I have selected from Robinson's very substantial body of work. They form the essential substance of this book, and need no defence from me.

It needs to be added that Robinson's longer poems are well worth exploring. I shall discuss them later, but they are far too long to include in what is really an initial introduction to this poet. All of them were written with the care and exactitude which was Robinson's habit. He wrote nothing simply for the sake of it, or to increase his literary reputation. The other *Selected Poems* included in my Bibliography contain a few poems of intermediate length, but none of them have room for the substantial long poems, most of which were published as separate volumes.

I

It's important to know where a poet comes from because much of the poet's work will in some way reflect those origins. In Robinson's case, this is particularly important. He came from the north eastern region of the United States, from the State of Maine, a part of the country which, like most American States, has its own cultural identity. Maine is the furthest north east of all the eastern States, and is tucked in between the mountains of Canada in the north and west, and the sea in the east. The eastern seabord stretches northwards into the Canadian State of New Brunswick and southwards to the border of the American State of New Hampshire. The people who lived in this area were lowland people, who regarded the mountains to their west not simply as a physical barrier but as a cultural barrier as well. Their interests were directed towards agriculture and fishing, and their lives were dominated by the society of village settlements and small towns. Their more substantial business interests were centred on construction work and timber, as well as commercial fish processing and the export of agricultural produce. The atmosphere of the eastern regions of the United Kingdom would not have been foreign to such people, and readers of Robinson can happily place him in such an environment. Norfolk and Lincolnshire, perhaps.

Robinson came from a place called Gardiner, which was then about the size of King's Lynn, in Norfolk or Boston in Lincolnshire and, like both, situated on a river. Again like King's Lynn and Boston, it was within easy each of the sea. Gardiner became 'Tilbury Town' in Robinson's poems, although *The Town Down the River*, the title of one of his collections, refers not to Gardiner but New York. Many of his poems centre on small-town life and local characters.

Robinson's family were solidly middle class, and prosperous, at least initially. His father was a merchant, and one of his brothers became a successful businessman. His other brother became a doctor. Edwin (a name he detested) was the youngest. Robinson's family were influential and well respected in the neighbourhood. Both his brothers were robust and sporting, but Robinson was aloof, and had no interest in sport or energetic social activities. He was very quiet, but very observant. And he was never really happy either. The way he was treated by his parents didn't improve matters. He always felt that his brothers were their favourites, while he was an awkward addition to the family. He once described his childhood as 'stark and unhappy'.

For a start, it was six months or so before he was even given a name. On top of that, his mother had wanted a girl and, for some time, dressed the toddler Robinson in girls' clothes. At that time, he had long curly hair to match. But he resented all this and when, at last, his parents selected a boy's name for him from a hat and he became 'Edwin', he inherited a name which did him no favours. Everyone called him 'Win', which was even worse. He always referred to himself as 'A.E.'.

But Robinson developed, even as a lonely child, a defiant pride in himself. He began writing poems at a very early age and continued to do so for the rest of his life. It was a skill which others were slow to respect, especially his family. To his father and mother, he was rather a nonentity in comparison with his brothers. Herman was his father's favourite, and primed to go into business with him, and Dean, his mother's, was heading for a career in medicine. Robinson, meanwhile, was engineering himself into Gardiner's small-town literary life, and building up a circle of friends who were interested in poetry. Amongst this particular cultural group, his talent was soon realised and respected, but there was little likelihood of it ever leading anywhere. The handsome and sports-loving Herman was encouraging his father in various business deals; Dean was at Maine Medical College; and Robinson was doing nothing in particular except writing poems. What was to be done with him?

Fortunately, after Robinson had graduated from High School, Herman persuaded his father to send Robinson to Harvard and, in spite of his father's lack of enthusiasm, Robinson was released from having to find some sort of a living in the town, having spent two years surviving on the family's wealth, which was fast diminishing. He needed treatment for a badly injured ear, which included a burst ear-drum. It was the result of physical punishment he had received at school. It troubled him all his life, and could possibly have increased his sense of social isolation. Anyway, there was enough money available for his father to send him to Harvard for a couple of years and, in the process, arrange for medical treatment in Boston.

Robinson had no interest in a career of any kind, and had not even been particularly academic at school, although he had a lively appreciation and workable knowledge of Latin. He had less Greek but learned French, German and Italian because he wanted to read the literature in those languages. He tended to work at anything which might further his obsessive interest in poetry. He was already working hard to perfect the poems that came easily from his pen. Harvard was the kind of environment which he needed, both to increase his potential readership, and to stimulate his intellect.

Gardiner had its own literary society, hardly different from the kind of local literary societies to be found throughout Britain. As happens here, amateur poets of various shapes and sizes gathered to read their poems to each other and to seek approval from fellow members. A local doctor was an active member of

Gardiner's literary society, and had poems regularly published in the local newspaper. Robinson showed him some of his poems, and the doctor recognised his talent. He introduced Robinson to various other local people with literary interests, as well as encouraging him to come to the literary society meetings. Robinson became something of a local star. From the age of seventeen until he left for Harvard at the age of twenty-one, he established himself as a person with literary ambitions. He had already had some local successes, and had even had a couple of poems published in the *Harvard Advocate* but, although only twenty-one, he was looking for wider and more significant recognition.

Boston was so utterly different from Gardiner, and Robinson immediately felt at home. Even in Gardiner, and while still at High School, Robinson had a small circle of friends. At High School, Robinson's friends were exclusively male. Although Robinson was seriously attracted to his brother Herman's wife, who was sympathetic to his literary ambitions, there is no evidence of his forming intimate friendships with the opposite sex. His male friends gathered to smoke, and to talk intensely about life and its problems. And this was the kind of circle Robinson was drawn to at Harvard as well. Although he was a 'special' student and not an official undergraduate, he was able to mix with men who were very different from his associates in a small, provincial town. These were men who had seen something of the world, who came from flourishing cities, who had received a sound academic education and had been brought up in a sophisticated and intellectual environment. Robinson moved freely among them, finding the kind of stimulation he had missed in Gardiner.

He developed the habit of staying up late, walking the streets, and having long conversations into the early hours, a way of living which persisted throughout his life. Friends were very important to him, and he was always loyal and generous towards them, as well as accepting help from them whenever he needed it. Much of his life was based on this reciprocal need, and, as a bachelor both by habit and by inclination, his friends were essential to any hopes of happiness. But in the kind of company he chose, he was mostly silent, except when he had drunk enough to loosen his emotional and intellectual frustrations. He was rarely noticeably drunk, however, and always marvellously coherent. He smoked continuously, cigarette after cigarette.

At Harvard, he enrolled in the classes that suited him: principally English, with the emphasis on Shakespearean studies, and French. He also did some Anglo-Saxon, but soon gave it up. He wasn't interested in competing academically with the other students, but was content to take what he wanted from the courses. As he wrote to a friend, 'B, and in that vicinity, is a very comfortable and safe place to hang.' But he did want to be noticed as a resident poet. In fact, two of his poems were published in the *Harvard Advocate* shortly after his arrival. He tried to insinuate himself into the company of those students who worked on the magazine, but he was too withdrawn and awkward to make a positive impression.

In 1893, Robinson left Harvard and returned to a family mired in difficult circumstances. His father died while his business was in Herman's hands. Herman had already begun to gamble the family assets in increasingly insecure projects and, over a relatively short period, had become an alcoholic. His brother, Dean, became addicted to laudanum while treating himself for neuralgia. Both brothers died relatively young, and both, with Robinson, witnessed their mother's horrific death from black diphtheria. The disease was so infectious that the doctor and the undertaker would not go in the house, while the pastor ministered from an open window. It was an experience Robinson would never forget.

He lived through all this and, at the same time, continued to write poetry in his own back room in the large family home. When he was not writing, he did whatever jobs were necessary around the house and garden: chopping wood, feeding the chickens, looking after the vegetables and fruit. Unknown to anyone else, he was already producing poems for which, in late middle age, he would become famous. Many of them had to wait for years before they were published. These four years, before he moved on, strengthened his vocation. Solitary, determined, convinced of his own worth as a poet but unrecognised by the literary world, he developed the kind of utter dedication which distinguished him from his more successful contemporaries. The miseries of his existence were transmuted into the strongest of poems, as was the frustration of being in love with his stricken brother's wife.

It has to be remembered that Robinson had had the serious intention of eventually marrying Emma Shepherd, the woman who became Herman's wife. He was very much in love with this beautiful woman, and she was sympathetic to his poetic aspirations, but he could not compete with his older brother, who was not only handsome, but socially confident, with a serious claim to a successful commercial career. For Emma, he seemed the sort of person who would provide both for her and her children. Robinson was not really in the running, but was deeply, and perhaps permanently, affected by her choice. Even when she had lost her husband, and was in desperate need of help, she refused, twice, Robinson's offer of marriage. He became a much-loved uncle to her children, and helped with money whenever he could.

Readers of Robinson need to remember all this, because his pessimism about love and marriage runs through much of his work. The close observation of married couples, combined with his memories of the marriages of his two brothers, seems to have convinced him of the impossibility of any kind of permanent happiness in married love.

In 1897 Robinson left Gardiner and made his home in New York. Apparently, this decision followed an argument with his brother Herman, overheard by Emma and the children. He went back to Gardiner from time to time, but he was more at home in the big city. He was no countryman, finding the countryside empty of the sort of human companionship he needed. He loved the noise, the streets packed with humanity, the cafes, the waterfront, the feeling of being within the heart of this restless mass. And he loved the nights, roaming from bar to bar, calling on new-made friends, talking into the early hours. The atmosphere stimulated his creative energies. But he was discouraged by the poor reception his first two privately published pamphlets received, although he had done his best to advertise their presence. No-one with any influence in the literary world responded to them with the kind of encouragement he wanted. But, in spite of that, he kept on writing, convinced of his worth

The details of Robinson's life can be followed in the biographies I have listed at the back of this book. But there are a few salient facts that need to be kept in mind when one reads his poems. First of all, he was, for many years, very poor. He borrowed from friends, he found what rented accomodation he could, and he often slept on the floors of already occupied apartments. The apartments which he found for himself were always dingy, dark, unprepossessing. He tramped up interminable metal staircases to what were often little more than cupboard-sized closets. He spent hours and hours in bars, and drinking in friends' apartments. He had no money for clothes and very little for anything else. What he did have was earned from casual labour or borrowed from friends. He would never commit himself to a permanent job, and had no interest in any career other than writing. He was generous when he had money, and his tastes were frugal. Cigarettes and alcohol were fortunately cheap. He knew, at first hand, what it was like to live amongst down-and-outs.

In 1904, he got his first break. He was thirty-five.

II

Although Robinson spent a lot of time with men who hung about in bars or cafes, or whom he met when he was doing various temporary jobs, most of them had nothing whatsoever to do with any kind of literary life. Robinson never forced himself on the company of others, but it was inevitable that some of the company he found himself in would include the odd literary aspirant or, more likely, failure. Unfortunately for him, even those literary acquaintances who became friends could do little to help him, consumed as they were with their own ambitions. Then, as these things sometimes happen, he had a stroke of luck.

A boy whose father happened to be President of the United States, came across Robinson's *Captain Craig*, which had recently been published by Houghton Mifflin in 1902, under pressure from friends who guaranteed its cost. No-one of any literary importance had taken any interest in the book, until a teacher showed it to Kermit Roosevelt. And Kermit shared his immediate enthusiasm with his father. Robinson had been ignored by the literary establishment, but no-one could afford to ignore the President of the United States, who was immediately struck by the quality of the poems.

Robinson, at this time, was in a very depressed state, and drinking heavily, discouraged by the poor reception of his book. His previous two books, *The Torrent and the Night Before* and *The Children of the Night*, had been little more than pamphlets, published by subscription. He had hoped that *Captain Craig* would receive literary recognition and introduce his work to a wider and significant readership. The silence was deafening.

Roosevelt, meanwhile was reading the book with great interest, and had no doubts about its literary worth. But when he made enquiries about its author, he found him difficult to trace. Eventually, however, he managed to get in touch with Robinson directly and offered to find him a post of some sort which would give him the financial security to get on with his writing. He made Robinson several offers which he was reluctant to accept. It is difficult not to be impressed by Robinson's integrity and dedication to his work which, in spite of his dire circumstances, he would never agree to compromise. In the end, however, after much persistence, Roosevelt managed to get Robinson to accept a post in the New York Customs House, on the understanding that the post would be very undemanding and not interfere with his vocation. The President also wrote an article for an influential journal, praising Robinson's poems, as well as getting Scribner's to republish the second of Robinson's pamphlets, *The Children of the Night.*

None of this, sadly, did much for Robinson's literary reputation. But, for five years, Robinson had somewhere to live and money to spend. In 1909, when Roosevelt was succeeded by Taft, who expected Robinson to be an efficient and dedicated Customs Officer, Robinson resigned. However, during these five years, Robinson managed to live a more stable and secure life than he had before. Up until 1902, he had been in despair. He was having to exist on casual labouring jobs and his failure to interest editors and publishers in his work had caused him to spend more and more time in downtown bars in the evenings, and often well into the night. He had also stopped writing poetry, but was writing plays instead. He wrote fiction, too. The fact that he now had money didn't mean that he immediately started writing poetry, but it did mean that his failures were slightly more bearable and he could comfort himself by trying other forms of literary activity. It needs to be remembered that Robinson was a naturally gifted writer. His letters are copious and beautifully written as, no doubt, was his fiction. But he was not easily marketable. He had literary friends, some of them influential, but he was too original to be fashionable.

But the poems had accumulated over the years, and a substantial number of them had never circulated. Those that had were returned to him by editor after editor and it is interesting to note that many of them were gathered together in *The Town Down the River*, which appeared in 1910, a year or so after his departure from the Customs House. Also included in the new volume were poems he had written at Gardiner, where poems had come more easily to him. He had been living there for much of 1909. *The Town Down the River* was dedicated to Theodore Roosevelt and Robinson was hopeful about its success.

It failed. There were one or two favourable reviews, but nothing on which to build any kind of literary reputation. However, Robinson had managed to accumulate a number of literary friends and was energetically continuing to write plays and fiction. None of this came to much, but it all softened the blow that literary rejection had dealt him. Later, he would destroy the lot.

It was Robinson's literary friends who pressed him to spend time in Peterborough, New Hampshire. There was a sort of artists' colony there, run by the MacDowells, a retired teacher with literary pretensions and his somewhat disabled wife. They had bought a farm way out in the country and established a home for writers and artists, not unlike the kind of place much favoured today here in Britain. Robinson began to spend his summers there, writing intensely and, at the same time, enjoying the countryside, shared evening meals, and the company of like-minded individuals. While there, he was free from the temptations of alcohol and was well looked after. But it was the kind of life he lived in New York which provided the ideas for his poems.

After her husband died, Mrs MacDowell continued to run the hostel. The sort of encouragement and help she gave Robinson was shared, throughout his life, by a number of women who were drawn to this odd, shy and retiring poet. In fact, although he spent much of his time in New York with various male friends, many of them bar-regulars and general hangers-on, he shared most of his sensitivities with women. They were generally married women, and it was to them he sent whatever poems he felt needed testing. There was Herman's wife, Emma; Laura Richards, who ran various groups from her large house; Edith Brower, who shared an intense correspondence with him; Josephine Peabody, a writer who found Robinson particularly attractive and wrote to him often; and Clara Davidge, a wealthy widow, who had a studio built for Robinson behind her large house in Washington Square. All these women were drawn to Robinson and gave him the sort of motherly protection he seems to have needed. But in every case, he was wary of becoming too dependent on them, and shied away from any kind of physical intimacy. But such was the case with all Robinson's friends. He seems to have set a high value on being free from any kind of permanent attachment. The only woman whom he had any thoughts of marrying was Emma, with whom he had been desperately in love, but who chose his brother Herman for a husband, and turned Robinson down even after her husband had died. These particular rejections seem to have had a permanent effect on Robinson.

The MacDowell colony in Peterborough, New Hampshire, established a place in Robinson's life like no other. His continuing presence there, beginning in 1911, when he was in his early forties, demonstrates how the security and comfort he found there, together with its stimulating artistic residents, enriched a life withered by disappointments. At the MacDowell colony Robinson found himself among creative people who sympathised with his problems, shared his creative enthusiasms, and provided him with company and good conversation whenever he needed it. In the daytime, he worked steadily at his poetry; in the evenings he could enjoy good food without feeling a desperate need for alcohol. At Peterborough, Robinson worked steadily summer after summer, but escaped regularly to Gardiner and New York and other such places to gather material for his poetry. As he had done throughout his life, he relied on friends for support and accommodation.

Gradually, almost imperceptibly, he began to find an audience for his work. The fiction had failed, the plays had failed, but the poetry was easing its way into places where influence mattered. As is often the case, from his first book onwards a small number of enthusiastic readers had steadily increased, in spite of his failure to excite the literary press. His friends, too, had been consistently loyal, and their number and influence was also growing.

By 1913 Robinson was getting into print more often, and what he wrote was being noticed in places where it mattered. He was 44, and much of his best work had already been written.

III

The Atlantic and *Poetry* both began to publish poems by Robinson, and Alfred Noyes, a famous English poet of the time, wrote a significant article about Robinson in the *Boston Evening Transcript*, claiming that he was the best American poet then writing. These things matter. However much individual readers claim for a poet, their influence is insignificant if their appreciation is not backed by writers who have real influence. That single article by Noyes may well have done more for Robinson's reputation that anything else than had been said and written about him. The publication of Robinson's fifth volume, *The Man Against the Sky*, in 1916, made his reputation. *The New Republic* printed a review by the most influential poetry editor of the time, Amy Lowell. This was a book 'of great power'. It was 'dynamic with experience and knowledge of life'. Although the book received a number of reviews, and although many of them were far less enthusiastic than Amy Lowell's, Robinson was at last being noticed, and it mattered to him more than anything else that he had experienced in over twenty years of writing life. He had become a poet to be reckoned with. He was to publish nineteen or so collections before his last *Collected Poems* was posthumously published in 1937, and this list included a *Collected Poems* in 1921, barely five years after the publication of *The Man Against the Sky*.

Robinson was prolific. He had always been prolific. But much of this creative energy had been wasted on fiction and play-writing, in an attempt to gain some kind of recognition. Now, such diversions were no longer necessary, and he was able to write poems which would be certain of a publisher. No doubt, this sense of having arrived encouraged him to think of getting together all his previous work and publishing it all in a *Collected Poems*. Such events are significant in the writing life of every poet, whether encouraged by a publisher or not. They represent a harvest of success: a body of work which is intended to establish itself as part of the living canon.

Strangely, this new success was accompanied by a new relationship with three women: Esther Bates, Elizabeth Marsh, and Mabel Daniels. All three were young and artistic, and all three were connected with the Peterborough colony. As with other young women there, they were all interested in exploring the inner life of this intensely shy but increasingly significant poet. They searched in his poems for possible clues, finding it intriguing that such a man had remained single and seemingly celibate for so long. Robinson was genuinely fond of the company of all three of them, and enjoyed periods of intense conversation, but he kept them all at a safe distance, no doubt increasing their curiosity in the process.

There is no doubt at all that Robinson enjoyed such friendships but, as in all his friendships, he was more of an interested spectator than an engaged participant. He had always been known for being completely silent in convivial company; something his friends had become used to. He almost never showed any depth of feeling in public. That is not to say that he was a person without sympathy. Quite the contrary. He was a much-loved uncle to Emma's children, for instance, and children are very penetrating in these matters. He was quite prepared to listen, and was known for this capacity. It was something closest friends valued in him. But he was never prepared to discuss his own work in public, and usually deflected references to it, or provided tangential and oblique responses to exploratory questions. He could even be quite flippant about it all.

But Robinson always insisted that his poems were him. If anybody wanted to know him then he was to be found in his poems. His other life, with all its customary routines and responsiblities, were of no particular interest, he felt. In fact, he reduced his responsibilities as much as he could in order to devote his life to writing poems. It was then, completely alone and often for hours at a time, that he released onto paper the urgencies that he consciously restrained in normal human intercourse. Not that his poems were obviously about himself. He almost never used the pronoun 'I' in his poems, except when it was clear that one of his characters was speaking. All his characters were, however, aspects of himself, and the romantic relationships explored in some of the poems were expressions of the feelings which he never openly communicated to individual women, except perhaps to Emma. But, in spite of that, Robinson appears able to explore these relationships in great depth, with extraordinary sensitivity.

And this was no doubt one of the reasons for his increasing readership in the years between 1916 and his death in 1935.

The main reason for Robinson's increasing popularity, however, was his increasing visibility. When a poet is regularly published and regularly reviewed, the reading public becomes familiar with the poet's presence in print and, almost by habit, tends to buy the poet's books. Nevertheless, it is important to realise the fact that Robinson is a very attractive poet in many ways, and his poems have none of the obscurity that accompanied more 'modernist' poems, especially novel and experimental work. Robinson was traditional in the best sense: employing verse forms and techniques that were to hand, and had always been available to a practising poet. An argument could be made that he became, for conservatives, an example of what was possible without being revolutionary or exotic; and that his obvious accomplishment with traditional forms showed just what could be done. At the same time, those who supported the 'modernist' cause were able to label him as 'yesterday's man': someone who lacked the kind of adventurous spirit necessary for original work.

Apparently, when someone asked Robinson why he didn't write in 'free verse', Robinson replied that he wrote 'badly enough as it is'. It was the kind of evasive answer that was his habit. These literary wars were of no interest to Robinson. What was being done in poetry appeared to him neither novel nor impressive. He was engaged in a communicative process which didn't have those kinds of boundaries. For him, there were forms enough already in existence. The problem was how to handle them to effectively communicate the pressures that he felt. He was always, and essentially, a craftsman, and one whose technical skills were equal to what he wanted to express. Whatever the circumstances, and however the lack of public acclaim, he was never uncertain about his poetic gifts.

For four months of every year, Robinson worked steadily at his poetry. Alone in his workshop at the MacDowell colony, he laboured intensively for hours at a time. He had breakfast at 7.30, then took a walk in the woods before returning to his studio and working until lunchtime. His lunch was left outside his door. He worked on through the afternoon until it was time for him to appear at the communal dinner. The others always noticed and often commented on his silence, but he was more amused by this than agitated. He played pool, listened to any musical recitals that were laid on, and sometimes read a detective novel. Sometimes, he played cards. From time to time, there were discussions before the fire until late into the night.

According to one of his biographers (Hermann Hagedorn) there was once a discussion about the financial returns for writing poetry, and Robinson said, 'If the Chief of Police knew how much money I have made on poetry during the past twenty-five years, I would be arrested for vagrancy'. Someone commented that if he advertised himself more he might be a best-seller. Robinson replied, 'No, you're wrong there. There are not enough people who would know what I am saying, even if they did read me. A poet's trade is a martyr's trade.' And, apparently, when a female friend suggested she might write his biography, he said, 'Make sure you say to these people who say I gave up great things to write poetry, that there was only one thing in the world I could give up, and that was writing poetry, for that was all that meant anything to me.'

Robinson's companions at the MacDowell colony included many young writers, male and female, and some of them went on to achieve considerable success. As they became more well-known, they carried with them the friendship of an increasingly well-known older poet. By this sort of filtering process, Robinson's name and reputation spread through influential literary circles. Younger poets brought him their work, hoping for advice and encouragement. One of them was the poet Robert Frost, who was later to write a review of Robinson's last book, *King Jasper*, which Robinson finished editing from his deathbed. Robinson's influence on Frost's poetry is everywhere evident, but has not yet been subject to critical analysis in any depth.

In 1919, on his fiftieth birthday, the *New York Times Review of Books* carried a headline which said, POETS CELEBRATE E.A. ROBINSON'S BIRTHDAY. Amy Lowell wrote in *The Dial*, 'If a contemporary dare to say that any living writer is sure to rank among the most important poets of his nation, I dare to say this of Mr Robinson.' His *Collected Poems* (1921) received the Pulitzer Prize for poetry. Yale gave him an honorary degree. Robinson had arrived.

IV

There was a price to pay for eventual fame. A modern reader thumbing through the final *Collected Poems* is immediately put off by the long poems which almost coincide with Robinson's increasing popularity. From *Avon's Harvest*, published in 1921 until *King Jasper*, his final book, almost all of Robinson's poems were of some length. In fact, he tended to publish these long poems as separate books. *Avon's Harvest* begins on page 543 of the 1937 *Collected Poems* and there are a further 945 pages of reading. Enough to intimidate even the most enthusiastic of readers. It seems that Robinson somehow felt that he had to justify his new reputation by producing a substantial quantity of work. Since he chose not to do any other work other than writing poems, even to the extent of refusing to write reviews or teach, he had time on his hands. Not only that, he may have intended to jealously guard his new reputation.

One of the obvious ways of being noticed as a poet is to produce a substantial body of work, and it has, perhaps, become customary to regard a substantial body of work as a significant sign of what is called a 'major' or 'great' poet. This is particularly unfortunate since what might be called 'poetic power' or simply 'creativity' declines with age. Readers of English poetry, especially those who have to read poetry as part of their studies, soon become aware of the sheer volume of the poetry that faces them. A good dose of *The Fairie Queene* or *Paradise Lost* has intimidated many an otherwise able student.

But is this just a matter of volume, or length? One notices, in bookshops, works of fiction which might seem, to some, of inordinate length. Yet avid readers of fiction appear to have an appetite for such books; indeed, to feel deprived when they are offered anything shorter. Nevertheless, it is reasonable to assume that there are other readers who find the longer works of fiction tedious to plough through. What did poetry readers of Robinson's day expect?

Before we try to decide on this question, we have to bear in mind the literary climate determined by publishers, editors, and literary journalists. We cannot read work which is unavailable. If publishers are unwilling to publish it, then what hope is there of ever coming across it except, possibly, in obscure and very limited places. And publishing, being a business, relies on assessing what the current literary climate will find acceptable. Hence the need for publishers to consult specialist readers and familiarise themselves with what is already in the market, as well as absorbing current fashions from reviews and the media. So, the question of what readers of Robinson expected was, in a sense, what they got. So, what did they get?

First of all, they got substance. Before the advent of radio and television, reading was one of the primary ways of spending one's leisure and with the increase of leisure came the appetite for longer books. The minority who could read in the sixteenth and seventeenth centuries had the leisure to read Spenser and Milton, and a far narrower range of choice than in our own day. But much later, in Victorian times, there was mental and physical space for the long poem. At the end of the nineteenth century and into the early twentieth century, long poems still thrived, although there was an increasing tendency to prefer shorter lyrics to long narrative poems.

Robinson certainly seems to have preferred writing short poems in the days when he was relatively unknown. This, no doubt, coincided with the general attitude to poetry which he then held. He read Browning and he read Crabbe but, until later in life, he chose not to emulate them. His taste appears to have leaned more towards Hardy and Kipling, who had the gift of writing powerful lyrics. Kipling, particularly, has the kind of energy which is characteristic of Robinson's lyrics. And this kind of energy is peculiar to young poets, whose creative powers are more immediate and spontaneous. We see this in the case of both Wordsworth and Coleridge, and with the Romantics generally. Both declined in what we might call 'poetic energy' as they aged. When that kind of energy fades in a poet, it is replaced by the stamina required to produce longer poems. Poets appear to have a choice: either to accept this loss of spontaneous energy and stop writing poems, or manufacture longer work to consolidate their reputations.

It seems that this happened with Robinson. What he had to say about poetry was recorded when he was an established poet. Nobody would have asked a younger Robinson what his opinions were. In fact, the younger Robinson was probably too busy actually getting down the poems which came to him rather than ruminating on the process. But I think it is a mistake for a critic as eminent as the American critic Yvor Winters to play down what one might call the 'inspirational element' in the younger Robinson, simply because of an aversion to the 'Romantic' idea of poetry. Winters found Robinson's technical qualities attractive, and attributed them to the kind of mental discipline he applied to his own poems. However, the poems which Winters wrote lack the kind of energetic power which is a distinguishing feature of Robinson's shorter poems.

It seems to me that the American reading public missed the qualities of Robinson's early poems simply because the poems were largely unavailable, and because Robinson had no inclination to publicise himself nor the reviewers to promote him. The Robinson who 'arrived' hadn't changed. But the attitude of publishers and reviewers had. Robinson had suddenly become fashionable.

Sadly, as the influence of 'modernism' increased and literary fashion changed with it, Robinson slowly became unfashionable, and his longer poems even more so. In Britain, Robinson has been unpublished and ignored. The literary establishment in this country operates in exactly the same way as it does in the United

States, and with the same kind of insularity. British academics and literary critics have been unadventurous in their search for overlooked talent, and publishers have followed suit. Anthologists, too, have leaned too heavily on established opinion. Yet Robinson, by any standards, is an exciting, enjoyable, invigorating, and stimulating poet. However, such judgements need to be defended. It is time to look more closely at the poems themselves.

V

Normally, suggesting that a reader look at a poem or two by a particular poet simply involves opening the nearest anthology. In Robinson's case this is particularly unproductive: Robinson has almost never been anthologised in this country. And as I have suggested, the odd reader who comes across his *Collected Poems* will be discouraged by its solidity and weight from further exploration. Again, anyone who opens the book is likely to open it in the middle of one of the several long poems which crowd the later pages. But what are these long poems like?

Eleven of Robinson's books are single-poem books. Three of these are what might be called 'Arthurian' poems, all related in some way to the tales in Malory's fifteenth-century translation of *Morte d'Arthur* from the French. Tennyson did something similar in his *Morte d'Arthur*, and this might be a good occasion to compare the poetic styles of the two poets. In Tennyson's poem, the King is admonishing Sir Bedivere for not hurling the sword, Excalibur, into the Lake at his command:

> 'Thou hast betray'd thy nature and thy name,
> Not rendering true answer, as beseem'd

Thy fealty, nor like a noble knight:
For surer sign had follow'd, either hand,
Or voice, or else a motion of the mere.
This is a shameful thing for men to lie.
Yet now, I charge thee, quickly go again
As thou art lief and dear, and do the thing
I bade thee, watch, and lightly bring me word.'

And here is Robinson's King Arthur, admonishing Bedivere and Gawaine for expecting more from him:

'You, Bedivere,
And you, Gawaine, are shaken with events
Incredible yesterday, – but kings are men.
Take off their crowns and tear away their colours
And let them see with my eyes what I see –
Yes, they are men, indeed! If there's a slave
In Britain, with a reptile at his heart
Like mine that with his claws of ice and fire
Tears out of me the fevered roots of mercy,
Find him, and I will make a king of him.'

When using Malory's material, Robinson is interested in the relations between people: between the knights and King Arthur, and between King Arthur and Guinevere, as well as between Guinevere and Lancelot. Tennyson is less interested in psychology than in creating a sort of medieval atmosphere. And Tennyson generally, in other poems, chooses to create moods rather than emotional complexity. At his most intense, say in *In Memoriam*, he still uses nature to give power to his mood of desolation, relying on visual image to give the poem substance. We know nothing of Arthur Hallam from reading the poem. Robinson would certainly have made his relationship with Hallam the centre of such a poem and, strangely, in comparison with Tennyson, Robinson was never self-indulgent about his own feelings. We would have learnt a great deal about Arthur Hallam and far less about the poet himself.

Generally, Robinson's blank verse is less varied metrically than Tennyson's but gets much closer to the colloquial. Reading through the Robinson quotation above, variety in pace is evident, created by fine technical skill in maintaining a basic pentameter stress pattern, with the odd variation. Tennyson's blank verse, however, loses pace by preferring the archaic to the colloquial. Tennyson's long poems maintain our interest because of his fine ear, and his ability to create atmosphere and mood through patterned variations in rhythm. Robinson does this in his short poems but relies on the complexity of human relations in his long poems. In other words, Robinson's long poems are interesting because of what they say rather than how they say it. Although Robinson never wrote long poems in heroic couplets, like Crabbe, any interest in Robinson's long poems would be similar to a reader's interest in Crabbe's.

The themes in Robinson's long poems are mostly those of human relationships, especially those between men and women. Also involved are power struggles, human jealousy and betrayal, the difference between youth and age, innocence and experience, sickness and death. The problem for the reader is not just the inordinate length of the poems, but their obliquity. Robinson is fond of rumination, in a manner which reminds one of Emerson, and even more of Henry James. The reader often gets lost in what seems tangential and irrelevant to the narrative. This is never the fault of the shorter poems. Perhaps a quote from one of the longer poems might give the flavour. Here is a section from *The Man Who Died Twice*:

Like shining grain
Long fouled and hidden by chaff and years of dust
In a dark place, and after many seasons
Winnowed and cleaned, with sunlight falling on it,
His wits were clear again. He had no power
To use them, and at first repudiated
The faintest wakening flicker of any wish
For use of any such power. But a short fight
Found his whole fragile armour of negation
So tattered that it fell away from him
Like time-worn kingly rags of self-delusion
At the rough touch of the inevitable –
Till he confessed a rueful willingness
To reason that with time and care this power
Would come, and coming might be used.

This is more than competent verse, but the reader loses the sense of narrative by becoming lost, in a Jamesian sense, in fine psychological and emotional detail. It takes a cerain kind of stamina and intellectual interest in a reader to maintain concentration over seventy or eighty pages, or even more, of such writing. This is not to say the long poems are hardly worth reading. For a reader who has made a habit of reading longer poems and who gets considerable pleasure from them, Robinson's long poems promise hours of pleasure. The writing is rhythmically controlled and fluent, and can be very moving. The subject matter is mentally and emotionally absorbing, and always of philosophical and psychological interest, but the taste for such writing has to be uncommon.

There are a number of poems, however, which are of medium length and well worth looking at. The best are 'Rembrandt to Rembrandt', 'Ben Jonson entertains a man from Stratford', 'Aunt Imogen', 'Isaac and Archibald' and 'The Three Taverns'.

'Rembrandt to Rembrandt' is an exploration of artistic integrity, as the painter cross-examines his self-portrait. He questions not only his honesty but the honesty in the painting. In the writing of this poem, Robinson questions his own integrity as a poet, and his vocation to speak the truth as he sees it, irrespective of public acclaim or condemnation. Rembrandt says to his painting:

> There's life in you that shall outlive my clay
> That's for a time alive and will in time
> Be nothing – but not yet. You that are there
> Where I have painted you are safe enough,
> Though I see dragons.

Robinson shows Rembrandt as an artist driven by demons and controlled by forces which it would be suicide to ignore:

> Since I am but a living instrument
> Played on by powers that are invisible.

The point of the poem is that the old, poor and neglected Rembrandt is the same Rembrandt who was once young and rich and famous, and the paintings reflect the artistic integrity and devotion of the man who painted them. It is the truth in them which is incorruptible and gives them value and life. Robinson could write so well about this because he himself suffered years of neglect but always believed in the integrity of his work.

'Ben Jonson Entertains A Man From Stratford' is not unlike the Rembrandt poem in both manner and theme. In this case, it's the mystery of the ordinary man Shakespeare, from whose imagination came such vastness, complexity, and passion: whole worlds where men and women laughed, loved and died, where rivals fought, where nations collided, and where audiences were caught up in lives that seemed more real than their own. Who was this man? Ben Jonson is curious to find out what one of the locals thought about one of their own, hoping to find out, perhaps, what the real Shakespeare was like as a man. Once again we have the seeming incongruity between the artist as ordinary human being and the artist as someone from whom comes these other worlds. Robinson himself was never really able to reconcile these two aspects of himself. He was most himself when he was busy writing, but what was he expected to do for the rest of the time? From what little we know of Shakespeare's life, he seems to have been sensible and practical, and perfectly happy to retire comfortably in Stratford on the wealth he had carefully managed from his writing. Ben Jonson knew him as a friend and drinking companion, but still wondered how such a man could live two lives:

> Yes, he'll go back to Stratford. And we'll miss him?
> Dear sir, there'll be no London here without him.
> We'll all be riding, one of these fine days,
> Down there to see him – and his wife won't like us ...

Ben Jonson was astonished by the fertility of Shakespeare's imagination, and enthralled by his talk. But, at the same time, he was unnerved by it all:

> When he talks like that,
> There's nothing for a human man to do
> But lead him to some grateful nook like this
> Where we be now, and there to make him drink.
> He'll drink for love of me, and then be sick;
> A sad sign always in a man of parts.
> And always very ominous.

Robinson himself spent many hours in convivial company, and remained for the most part silent. He needed more than an average quantity of alcohol before he finally opened up. He found his own inability to converse easily, his own self-identity, strange. The way he tries to penetrate the mystery of Shakespeare's identity in this poem is, in essence, an exploration of the mystery of himself. He always does this not by obvious self-reflection. He rarely uses the personal pronoun 'I' in his poems. He is immensely curious about other people because, through them, he can live other parts of himself.

'Isaac and Archibald' is little more than a man's memory of two old men who featured in his childhood, but Robinson writes with real affection of these two, and of their rather prickly relationship with each other. Now older, Robinson ruminates on the theme of ageing and death, and the rhythm and tone of the poem reminds one of Robert Frost, who must have picked it up from reading Robinson. The closing lines are particularly Frost-like:

> Isaac and Archibald have gone their way
> To the silence of the loved and well-forgotten.
> I knew them, and I may have laughed at them;
> But there's a laughing that has honour in it,
> And I have no regret for light words now.
> Rather I think sometimes they may have made
> Their sport of me; – but they would not do that,
> They were too old for that. They were old men,
> And I may laugh at them because I knew them.

'Aunt Imogen' is an intensely readable poem about a favourite aunt with a secret past, who loves and is much loved by the small children in the family:

> There was the feminine paradox – that she
> Who had so little sunshine for herself
> Should have so much for others.

Robinson suggests the sadness and unfulfillment of Aunt Imogen's life by the lightest of touches, and with fine delicacy.

> She knew that she could seem to make them all
> Believe there was no other part of her
> Than her persistent happiness; but the why
> And how she did not know.

It is the intensity of love that the children have for her that frees her from her own secret sadness. We are never told the cause of this sadness, but the very fact that she lives another lonely life, unmarried and companionless runs, like an undercurrent, through the poem. Again, Robinson himself lived such a life as a bachelor who needed his friends more, perhaps, than they needed him, and who was devoted to his grandchildren.

'The Three Taverns' is a poem in which St Paul gives an account of his life and his justification for it to his close companions. He is making his final journey to Rome. Once again, it is worth reading this poem with Robinson himself in mind. Paul insists on Faith, and the significance of the words he speaks in faith:

> If I have loosed
> A shaft of language that has flown sometimes
> A little higher than the hearts and heads
> Of nature's minions, it will yet be heard,
> Like a new song that waits for distant ears.
> I cannot be the man that I am not;
> And while I own that earth is my affliction,
> I am a man of earth, who says not all
> To all alike.

The poem has great power, and is written with extraordinary fluency, both in line and measure. It is, perhaps, one of the finest of Robinson's poems:

> As long as there are glasses that are dark –
> And there are many – we see darkly through them;
> All which I have conceded and set down
> In words that have no shadow.

One senses all the way through the poem the sureness of vocation which Robinson affirms through the character of Paul. His imaginative empathy with Paul's character and inner strength, and the sheer doggedness of Paul's faith, was possible because Robinson shared the inner conviction that his life was driven by impulses too strong to resist. But it is impossible to describe the power and inspirational vision which charges this poem.

>   Many with ears
> That hear not yet, shall have ears given to them,
> And then they shall hear strangely. Many with eyes
> That are incredulous of the Mystery
> Shall yet be driven to feel, and then to read
> Where language has an end and is a veil,
> Not woven of our words.

Fine though the longer poems of Robinson are, it is the shorter poems which make immediate and unforgettable impact. The opening lines of 'Luke Havergal' have only to be read once for them to echo forever through one's auditory imagination. And poem after poem lodges permanently in one's memory. Philip Larkin used to say that a poem needed to have a tune to make it the real thing, and no-one could possibly maintain that Robinson's shorter poems are tuneless. Robinson was very fond of Hardy's poems, as was Philip Larkin who made a habit of reading them every day. There is no evidence that Robinson stole any of Hardy's tunes, though, any more than Larkin did. However, it is claimed that Robinson stole tunes from the poet William Mackworth Praed, who died in 1839, and though 'stole' would be the wrong word, he had obviously read Praed and some of the tunes had remained in his memory. The argument is clearly presented by Yvor Winters in his book on Robinson, and is based on scholarly evidence provided by a certain Professor Hoyt Hudson. But there is little point in taking this further. The tone of Robinson's poems is quite different from that of the flippant Praed, and Robinson puts these tunes to quite different purposes. An over concentration on such matters detracts from the value of Robinson as a dedicated and serious poet, with intentions quite different from a versifier like Praed. Winters presents this argument in great detail, and uses exact textual references to substantiate his point. What he has to say about Robinson always has some interest, but Winters' efforts to present Robinson as a 'great' poet, however well argued, can become somewhat ponderous.

The fact is, Robinson's shorter poems have an immediate effect on any reader with an ear for verse. That effect is achieved because of Robinson's skill in choosing tunes which strike the reader as both unusual and hypnotic and, once caught in the spell, Robinson is able to engage the reader's absolute attention by presenting characters whose intrinsic interest excites the reader's imaginative sympathy. All poetry readers of whatever age and background are attracted to poetry because of its music and, from its beginnings, poetry has always been associated with song. In fact, a good case can be made that much modern poetry has moved so far away from its origins that much of it is no longer recognizable as poetry.

Robinson has, perhaps, been ignored because he chose to use traditional verse forms rather than experiment with free verse. But he was in fact able, in spite of this, to explore the emotional, and psychological aspects of his complex characters, as well as their personal relationships, with subtlety and fine sensitivity. His short poems are interesting because they are about real people in real situations. He is particularly good at creating female characters, and portrays them with great insight and sensitivity. In fact, more than a tenth of the poems in this selection are either about individual women or about their relationship with a man. His men are perhaps simpler creations but, nevertheless, dramatically present. We get to know Luke Havergal, Richard Cory, Reuben Bright, John Gorham and the rest of Robinson's male characters until they become almost familiars. Take Reuben Bright, for instance.

Reuben Bright was a butcher, whose wife has unexpectedly been diagnosed as terminally ill. We are told none of the details, but we are told how it affected Reuben when he was told. He 'stared at them' and burst into tears, but he also 'shook with fright'. Then, after his wife had been buried, he gathered all his wife's things together and burned them, and also 'tore down the slaughter house'. None of this is made much of. The poem has only two stanzas. Neither Reuben nor his wife are described, nor is their house. We have no setting really, and have no idea where all this takes place and what the area looks like. We only have a few stark facts about Reuben's reaction. Yet, strangely, we feel what kind of man he is: emotionally dependent on his wife, hard-working, unable to express his emotions easily, taciturn but subject to violent passion, blunt and single-minded. And we also feel his hurt at what has happened. Robinson presents all this in an almost casual, off-hand way, letting the facts speak for themselves. He makes no personal comment.

John Gorham is the victim of a woman, Jane Wayland, who has tormented him in the past and now taunts and teases him. The dialogue between him and Jane is intensified by the rhythm of the poem and the way that rhythm echoes the mocking tone of their voices. It gives Jane the room to play on John's sensitivities by saying 'you are sorry when you're not' and this is no time for 'long faces in the moonlight'. The couple are in a romantic setting, but the feelings they have are quite contrary to what might be expected. The poem concentrates on the bitterness John feels. Jane, on the other hand, says that John is making a fuss about nothing and is refusing to face up to reality: 'Won't you ever see me as I am, John Gorham' because 'Somewhere in me there's a woman if you know the way to find her'. Readers, eavesdropping on this very private quarrel, are left to make their own personal judgements of the wrongs and rights of it all. Robinson stands back, as he always does, in the shadows. It's as if he means to say: this is how it is, and this is life, and there is no more to be said about it. The focus is on the complex reality rather than any solution.

The same unflinching look at reality is found in 'The Woman and the Wife'. It is important to realise that Robinson never generalises. His poems are about specific characters in particular situations and circumstances. And in this poem he explores the nature of the husband's emotional needs and the wife's inability to provide him with the security that he wants. 'Let us both be strong,' she says, and accept unhappiness as a fact of life. She presses the husband not to 'throw yourself away because you love me'. Whatever hurt the husband has experienced, he should be true to the love he feels and be honest with his wife about 'what you miss'. Throughout the poem there runs the impossibility of perfect love between these two people, which they have to face. The woman urges the man to be constant in his love, even if the very constancy of their marriage compromises it. In what is a relatively short poem of under thirty lines, Robinson has created the sadness and frustration which can exist at the heart of married love. The woman asks the man to accept the impossibility of taking 'moonlight for the sun' and to give up seeing 'More marriage in the dream of one dead kiss' than the actual situation, where 'Passion has turned the lock'. But, as so often with Robinson, it is what is not said which gives the poem that extra power. There is never a suggestion in Robinson that the poem is more than life itself.

Robinson normally makes no attempt to judge his characters. He passes no judgement, for instance, on Miniver Cheevy, another man who refuses to face reality. Robinson, throughout his life, was close to men who were, in a sense, lost: they found life confusing, they had no particular aims, or even ideals, and they consoled themselves by drinking. They were, in common parlance, 'useless layabouts'. But not to Robinson. He never claimed to understand why people were as they were, and he never claimed the right to judge them.

Miniver Cheevy, however, is every one of us, however complacent and satisfied with ourselves we might be, and however successful we might appear. As with all of us at times, Miniver Cheevy considered 'life', and 'thought and thought and thought' about it. But he could make no sense of it. He 'called it fate, And kept on drinking'. Both Pound and Frost, by the way, found that extra 'thought' masterly.

Because Robinson gave formal shape to his poems, and never subscribed to the modern preference for free verse, he became neglected and, perhaps, regarded as lightweight. The same critical strictures have been applied to poets like John Betjeman. It is assumed that modern rhymed poems which rely on metre and formal verse structure must, necessarily, lack seriousness. So Eliot, for instance, chose rhymed verse for his *Old Possum's Book of Practical Cats* to differentiate those verses from his more serious work. Robinson, however, proves that serious poetry can be written in traditional forms. Robert Frost adopts a similar stance and he once made clear, in his review of Robinson's last long poem *King Jasper*, that 'Robinson stayed content with the old-fashioned way to be new.' It couldn't have been better put.

What we might call 'metrics' is too complex a subject to consider in detail here. Again, Robert Frost spoke well on this subject when he described the way a poet could write metrical verse without rigidly sticking to the metre: the metre was in the background rather than in the foreground. Shakespeare, for example, wrote the verse in his plays in iambic pentameters but, reading the verse, the rhythms of ordinary speech play over and against the metre. So, the lines can be read quantitively, although to do so distorts the natural speech rhythms. In fact, strictly quantitive measures in English verse are signs of poor quality writing. A good poet, like Robinson, is never confined by mechanical quantitive metre. In the same way, a jazz soloist is able to play close to and away from the rhythms followed by drummer and double bass. This sort of syncopation contributes to the pleasure the listener gets, and demonstrates the creativity of the performing artist. The same goes for poetry.

Linguists prefer to use the word 'measure' when discussing prosody, and this is helpful because it releases us from the referential restriction of the term 'metre' which, although appropriate for the discussion of Latin prosody, is hardly appropriate for a language like English. The idea of feet remains, and it is difficult to talk about English poetry without mentioning, for example, iambic pentameters, but this can obscure the skill with which a poet like Robinson plays upon the measure of the line. The line is played against a metrical background, but the accents of individual words and the movement of stresses within the line, together with the alliterative effect of consonantal clusters and the use of sophisticated rhyme schemes, creates a complex music which takes us far from the underlying metrical framework. It is difficult to illustrate this without very detailed examination of individual poems, but a comparison between 'The Poor Relation' and 'The House on the Hill', two very different poems, might demonstrate Robinson's technical range.

'The Poor Relation' is a complex poem, whereas 'The House on the Hill' seems comparatively simple. However, the apparent simplicity of 'The House on the Hill' is deceptive. The most obvious difference is the stress pattern: four stresses to the line in 'The Poor Relation' and three stresses to the line in 'The House on the Hill'. The faster tempo in the first poem is partly created by the stress being nearer the beginning of the line, whereas the slower tempo of the second is partly created by moving the first stress further into the line and making the last two stresses heavy and creating a pause at the end of the lines, slowing the flow. With 'The Poor Relation', the faster pace allows the line to run over into the next line more easily, although the pace is paused at the end of the rhyme completions, which have considerable control over the poem. The rhyme scheme in this poem is complex: *ab, ab, cc, ab*. It's important to notice the way Robinson contrasts and balances monosyllabic and polysyllabic rhymes: the *b* rhymes are essentially disyllabic but there is variation effected by the subtle use of unstressed grammatical words and the natural play within the rhyme itself. There are no simple, monosyllabic *b* rhymes in this poem, even where the main element of the rhyme is a monosyllabic noun or verb. The *a* rhymes, on the other hand, are relatively simple, and steady the movement of the verse. The *cc* rhymes provide a platform for the last two lines, so that the final line can bring into play the important *b* rhyme ending.

The rhyming in 'The House on the Hill' is very simple, and most of the rhyming words are monosyllabic. This gives Robinson the chance to make the *a* rhymes dominant, moving to the final *a* couplet at the end of the final stanza. Simplicity and directness are also achieved by a plain diction. The first and last lines of the first stanza are repeated three more times throughout the poem, forming alternately the last line of each stanza. The only irregular line in the poem is the second line of the last stanza, and it is purposely so, since it serves to break the steady movement of the previous stanzas in order to give the last two lines more emphasis.

To give a final and necessarily brief example of Robinson's technical skill, we can look at the first three stanzas of his 'Vickery's Mountain':

> Blue in the west the mountain stands,
>   And through the long twilight
> Vickery sits with folded hands,
>   And Vickery's eyes are bright.

Bright, for he knows what no man else
　　On earth as yet may know:
There's a golden word that he never tells,
　　And a gift that he will not show.

He dreams of honour and wealth and fame,
　　He smiles, and well he may;
For to Vickery once a sick man came
　　Who did not go away.

Each stanza contains four regularly stressed lines: four stresses followed by three stresses, twice repeated. The rhyme scheme is also simple: *ab*, *ab*. But Robinson counterpoints the formal stress pattern by moving the accents. For example, the second line of the first stanza has the three stresses, but the second stress has been affected by the heavy accent on the first syllable of the word 'twilight', a word of two syllables instead of one. If the phrase had been 'the length of night', the line would have been completely regular. The repetition of the word 'bright' at the beginning of the second stanza means that the rhythm of that line hangs on that first word. Stresses tend to fall on nouns, adjectives and adverbs, but not normally on prepositions or what are called 'grammatical words'. Again, if we compare the beginning of each of the three stanzas, the beginning of the third ('He dreams') necessitates a movement of the stress to 'dreams', whereas the stress is on the first word in the two previous stanzas. And, finally, notice the difference between the beginnings of the third lines of each stanza and the effect of the introduction of 'that' in the second stanza. It's these subtle variations in stressing and accent in colloquial speech which play against the artificiality of the verse form. Robinson's modulations are the result of unobtrusive but very fine technical skill.

And Robinson is masterly anyway. A poem like 'Hillcrest' moves with the kind of fluent power that one associates with the very best poems. Robinson is contemplating the effect of a writer's sanctuary, which Mrs MacDowell has provided (and to whom the poem is dedicated) on a man with too many 'ruins and regrets'. Robinson was never a 'nature poet' and is little interested in scene-painting, but he does manage to create the atmosphere of the place: 'where now September makes an island in a sea of trees'.

> He may by contemplation learn
> A little more than what he knew,
> And even see great oaks return
> To acorns out of which they grew.

But the contemplative will not learn what can never be known in this uncertain life. What will be achieved is the kind of humility which is necessary if life is to be tolerated and accepted. For Robinson, we do not have the control over life which our arrogance sometimes convinces us that we might have. It is an essential part of maturity to see that, and to know it:

> He may, if he but listen well,
> Through twilight and the silence here,
> Be told what there are none may tell
> To vanity's impatient ear;
>
> And he may never dare again
> Say what awaits him, or be sure
> What sunlit labyrinth of pain
> He may not enter and endure.

However, absolute knowledge, or completely realised wisdom,

is given to no-one: Whatever wisdom is supposed to have come is 'all unfound':

> Or like a web that error weaves
> On airy looms that have a sound
> No louder now than fallen leaves.

A comparison with Tennyson's 'In Memoriam', which is also written in regular four-line stanzas (and this is a just comparison), demonstrates Robinson's ability to contain more complexity and depth in such a form than Tennyson can. Eliot regarded 'In Memoriam' as what he called 'a major poem' but a good argument could be made in favour of the much shorter Robinson poem. Tennyson was a poet of scenic description and accompanying moods (mostly maudlin), but Robinson was a poet who could never have achieved the simplicity of mind that Tennyson had. He is closer in that respect to Browning, but without Browning's robust optimism and complex posturing. Robinson seems, to me, finer than both.

Robinson enjoyed reading Browning, and the way he chose to focus on 'characters' is similar to Browning's, but Robinson's view of life was the opposite of Browning's optimism and secure Christian belief. Robinson was serious in a way that only a minority of poets are, even when his depiction of a character is clothed in almost buoyant rhythms. The rhythms are not callous or insensitive: they express a vitality without which there would be no life at all. Yet, bound by this vitality, his characters are enmeshed in circumstances over which they have little control: they are victims of themselves, as well as of fate.

Perhaps George Crabbe, another poet whose poems Robinson enjoyed, best exemplifies the poetic integrity Robinson aimed at.

Like Crabbe, Robinson wanted to tell the truth but, unlike Crabbe, he chose a varied and attractive way of presenting it. Crabbe is dour, and writes within the stylistic conventions of the eighteenth-century heroic couplet. But Robinson's poem 'George Crabbe' somehow epitomises the significance, as a poet, of Robinson himself. It will serve as an appropriate ending to this very short introduction to Robinson's poems:

Give him the darkest inch your shelf allows,
Hide him in lonely garrets, if you will, –
But his hard, human pulse is throbbing still
With the sure strength that fearless truth endows.
In spite of all fine science disavows,
Of his plain excellence and stubborn skill
There yet remains what fashion cannot kill,
Though years have thinned the laurel from his brows.

Whether or not we read him, we can feel
From time to time the vigour of his name
Against us like a finger for the shame
And emptiness of what our souls reveal
In books that are as altars where we kneel
To consecrate the flicker, not the flame.

POEMS

The text of these poems is taken from Edwin Arlington Robinson's *Collected Poems*, New York, The Macmillan Company, 1937. Although many of the poems have been reprinted in various selections, it seems best to rely on Robinson's own final editing of his poems.

MINIVER CHEEVY

Miniver Cheevy, child of scorn,
  Grew lean while he assailed the seasons;
He wept that he was ever born,
  And he had reasons.

Miniver loved the days of old
  When swords were bright and steeds were prancing;
The vision of a warrior bold
  Would set him dancing.

Miniver sighed for what was not,
  And dreamed, and rested from his labors;
He dreamed of Thebes and Camelot,
  And Priam's neighbors.

Miniver mourned the ripe renown
  That made so many a name so fragrant;
He mourned Romance, now on the town,
  And Art, a vagrant.

Miniver loved the Medici,
  Albeit he had never seen one;
He would have sinned incessantly
  Could he have been one.

Miniver cursed the commonplace
  And eyed a khaki suit with loathing;
He missed the medieval grace
  Of iron clothing.

Miniver scorned the gold he sought,
  But sore annoyed was he without it;
Miniver thought, and thought, and thought,
  And thought about it.

Miniver Cheevy, born too late,
  Scratched his head and kept on thinking;
Miniver coughed, and called it fate,
  And kept on drinking.

LUKE HAVERGAL

Go to the western gate, Luke Havergal,
There where the vines cling crimson on the wall,
And in the twilight wait for what will come.
The leaves will whisper there of her, and some,
Like flying words, will strike you as they fall;
But go, and if you listen she will call.
Go to the western gate, Luke Havergal –
Luke Havergal.

No, there is not a dawn in eastern skies
To rift the fiery night that's in your eyes;
But there, where western glooms are gathering,
The dark will end the dark, if anything:
God slays Himself with every leaf that flies,
And hell is more than half of paradise.
No, there is not a dawn in eastern skies –
In eastern skies.

Out of a grave I come to tell you this,
Out of a grave I come to quench the kiss
That flames upon your forehead with a glow
That blinds you to the way that you must go.
Yes, there is yet one way to where she is,
Bitter, but one that faith may never miss.
Out of a grave I come to tell you this –
To tell you this.

There is the western gate, Luke Havergal,
There are the crimson leaves upon the wall.
Go, for the winds are tearing them away, –
Nor think to riddle the dead words they say,
Nor any more to feel them as they fall;
But go, and if you trust her she will call.
There is the western gate, Luke Havergal –
Luke Havergal.

HILLCREST

To Mrs Edward MacDowell

No sound of any storm that shakes
Old island walls with older seas
Comes here where now September makes
An island in a sea of trees.

Between the sunlight and the shade
A man may learn till he forgets
The roaring of a world remade,
And all his ruins and regrets;

And if he still remembers here
Poor fights he may have won or lost, –
If he be ridden with the fear
Of what some other fight may cost, –

If, eager to confuse too soon.
What he has known with what may be,
He reads a planet out of tune
For cause of his jarred harmony, –

If here he venture to unroll
His index of adagios,
And he be given to console
Humanity with what he knows, –

He may by contemplation learn
A little more than what he knew,
And even see great oaks return
To acorns out of which they grew.

He may, if he but listen well,
Through twilight and the silence here,
Be told what there are none may tell
To vanity's impatient ear;

And he may never dare again
Say what awaits him, or be sure
What sunlit labyrinth of pain
He may not enter and endure.

Who knows today from yesterday
May learn to count no thing too strange:
Love builds of what Time takes away,
Till Death itself is less than Change.

Who sees enough in his duress
May go as far as dreams have gone;
Who sees a little may do less
Than many who are blind have done;

Who sees unchastened here the soul
Triumphant has no other sight
Than has a child who sees the whole
World radiant with his own delight.

Far journeys and hard wandering
Await him in whose crude surmise
Peace, like a mask, hides everything
That is and has been from his eyes;

And all his wisdom is unfound,
Or like a web that error weaves
On airy looms that have a sound
No louder now than falling leaves.

EROS TURANNOS

She fears him, and will always ask
   What fated her to choose him;
She meets in his engaging mask
   All reasons to refuse him;
But what she meets and what she fears
Are less than are the downward years,
Drawn slowly to the foamless weirs
   Of age, were she to lose him.

Between a blurred sagacity
   That once had power to sound him,
And Love, that will not let him be
   The Judas that she found him,
Her pride assuages her almost,
As if it were alone the cost, –
He sees that he will not be lost,
   And waits and looks around him.

A sense of ocean and old trees
   Envelops and allures him;
Tradition, touching all he sees,
   Beguiles and reassures him;
And all her doubts of what he says
Are dimmed with what she knows of days –
Till even prejudice delays
   And fades, and she secures him.

The falling leaf inaugurates
　　The reign of her confusion;
The pounding wave reverberates
　　The dirge of her illusion;
And home, where passion lived and died,
Becomes a place where she can hide,
While all the town and harbour side
　　Vibrate with her seclusion.

We tell you, tapping on our brows,
　　The story as it should be, –
As if the story of a house
　　Were told, or ever could be;
We'll have no kindly veil between
Her visions and those we have seen, –
As if we guessed what hers have been,
　　Or what they are or would be.

Meanwhile we do no harm; for they
　　That with a god have striven,
Not hearing much of what we say,
　　Take what the god has given;
Though like waves breaking it may be,
Or like a changed familiar tree,
Or like a stairway to the sea
　　Where down the blind are driven.

FOR A DEAD LADY

No more with overflowing light
Shall fill the eyes that now are faded,
Nor shall another's fringe with night
Their woman-hidden world as they did.
No more shall quiver down the days
The flowing wonder of her ways,
Whereof no language may requite
The shifting and the many-shaded.

The grace, divine, definitive,
Clings only as a faint forestalling;
The laugh that love could not forgive
Is hushed, and answers to no calling;
The forehead and the little ears
Have gone where Saturn keeps the years;
The breast where roses could not live
Has done with rising and with falling.

The beauty, shattered by the laws
That have creation in their keeping,
No longer trembles at applause,
Or over children that are sleeping;
And we who delve in beauty's lore
Know all that we have known before
Of what inexorable cause
Makes Time so vicious in his reaping.

MR FLOOD'S PARTY

Old Eben Flood, climbing alone one night
Over the hill between the town below
And the forsaken upland hermitage
That held as much as he should ever know
On earth again of home, paused warily.
The road was his with not a native near;
And Eben, having leisure, said aloud,
For no man else in Tilbury Town to hear:

'Well, Mr Flood, we have the harvest moon
Again, and we may not have many more;
The bird is on the wing, the poet says,
And you and I have said it here before.
Drink to the bird.' He raised up to the light
The jug that he had gone so far to fill,
And answered huskily: 'Well, Mr Flood,
Since you propose it, I believe I will.'

Alone, as if enduring to the end
A valiant armor of scarred hopes outworn,
He stood there in the middle of the road
Like Roland's ghost winding a silent horn.
Below him, in the town among the trees,
Where friends of other days had honored him,
A phantom salutation of the dead
Rang thinly till old Eben's eyes were dim.

Then, as a mother lays her sleeping child
Down tenderly, fearing it may awake,
He set the jug down slowly at his feet
With trembling care, knowing that most things break;
And only when assured that on firm earth
It stood, as the uncertain lives of men
Assuredly did not, he paced away;
And with his hand extended paused again:

'Well, Mr Flood, we have not met like this
In a long time; and many a change has come
To both of us, I fear, since last it was
We had a drop together. Welcome home!'
Convivially returning with himself,
Again he raised the jug up to the light;
And with an acquiescent quaver said:
'Well, Mr Flood, if you insist, I might.

'Only a very little, Mr Flood –
For auld lang syne. No more, sir; that will do.'
So, for the time, apparently it did,
And Eben evidently thought so too;
For soon amid the silver loneliness
Of night he lifted up his voice and sang,
Secure, with only two moons listening,
Until the whole harmonious landscape rang –

'For auld lang syne.' The weary throat gave out,
The last word wavered, and the song was done.

He raised again the jug regretfully
And shook his head, and was again alone.
There was not much that was ahead of him,
And there was nothing in the town below –
Where strangers would have shut the many doors
That many friends had opened long ago.

THE POOR RELATION

No longer torn by what she knows
And sees within the eyes of others,
Her doubts are when the daylight goes,
Her fears are for the few she bothers.
She tells them it is wholly wrong
Of her to stay alive so long;
And when she smiles her forehead shows
A crinkle that had been her mother's.

Beneath her beauty, blanched with pain,
And wistful yet for being cheated,
A child would seem to ask again
A question many times repeated;
But no rebellion has betrayed
Her wonder at what she has paid
For memories that have no stain,
For triumph born to be defeated.

To those who come for what she was –
The few left who know where to find her –
She clings, for they are all she has;
And she may smile when they remind her,
As heretofore, of what they know
Or roses that are still to blow
By ways where not so much as grass
Remains of what she sees behind her.

They stay a while, and having done
What penance or the past requires,
They go, and leave her there alone
To count her chimneys and her spires.
Her lip shakes when they go away,
And yet she would not have them stay;
She knows as well as anyone
That Pity, having played, soon tires.

But one friend always reappears,
A good ghost, not to be forsaken;
Whereat she laughs and has no fears
Of what a ghost may reawaken,
But welcomes, while she wears and mends
The poor relation's odds and ends,
Her truant from a tomb of years –
Her power of youth so early taken.

Poor laugh, more slender than her song
It seems; and there are none to hear it
With even the stopped ears of the strong
For breaking heart or broken spirit.
The friends who clamored for her place,
And would have scratched her for her face,
Have lost her laughter for so long
That none would care enough to fear it.

None live who need fear anything
From her, whose losses are their pleasure;
The plover with a wounded wing
Stays not the flight that others measure;
So there she waits, and while she lives,
And death forgets, and faith forgives,
Her memories go foraging
For bits of childhood song they treasure.

And like a giant harp that hums
On always, and is always blending
The coming of what never comes
With what has past and had an ending,
The City trembles, throbs, and pounds
Outside, and through a thousand sounds
The small intolerable drums
Of Time are like slow drops descending.

Bereft enough to shame a sage
And given little to long sighing,
With no illusion to assuage
The lonely changelessness of dying, –
Unsought, unthought-of, and unheard,
She sings and watches like a bird,
Safe in a comfortable cage
From which there will be no more flying.

THE HOUSE ON THE HILL

They are all gone away,
    The House is shut and still,
There is nothing more to say.

Through broken walls and gray
    The winds blow bleak and shrill:
They are all gone away.

Nor is there one today
    To speak them good or ill:
There is nothing more to say.

Why is it then we stray
    Around the sunken sill?
They are all gone away.

And our poor fancy-play
    For them is wasted skill:
There is nothing more to say.

There is ruin and decay
    In the House on the Hill:
They are all gone away,
There is nothing more to say.

MANY ARE CALLED

The Lord Apollo, who has never died,
Still holds alone his immemorial reign,
Supreme in an impregnable domain
That with his magic he has fortified;
And though melodious multitudes have tried
In ecstasy, in anguish, and in vain,
With invocation sacred and profane
To lure him, even the loudest are outside.

Only at unconjectured intervals,
By will of him on whom no man may gaze,
By word of him whose law no man has read,
A questing light may rift the sullen walls,
To cling where mostly its infrequent rays
Fall golden on the patience of the dead.

THE SHEAVES

Where long the shadows of the wind had rolled,
Green wheat was yielding to the change assigned;
And as by some vast magic undivined
The world was turning slowly into gold.
Like nothing that was ever bought or sold
It waited there, the body and the mind;
And with a mighty meaning of a kind
That tells the more the more it is not told.

So in a land where all days are not fair,
Fair days went on till on another day
A thousand golden sheaves were lying there,
Shining and still, but not for long to stay –
As if a thousand girls with golden hair
Might rise from where they slept and go away.

THE VOICE OF AGE

She'd look upon us, if she could,
As hard as Rhadamanthus would;
Yet one may see, – who sees her face,
Her crown of silver and of lace,
Her mystical serene address
Of age alloyed with loveliness, –
That she would not annihilate
The frailest of things animate.

She has opinions of our ways,
And if we're not all mad, she says, –
If our ways are not wholly worse
Than others, for not being hers, –
There might somehow be found a few
Less insane things for us to do,
And we might have a little heed
Of what Belshazzar couldn't read.

She feels, with all our furniture,
Room yet for something more secure
Than our self-kindled aureoles
To guide our poor forgotten souls;
But when we have explained that grace
Dwells now in doing for the race,
She nods – as if she were relieved;
Almost as if she were deceived.

She frowns at much of what she hears,
And shakes her head, and has her fears;
Though none may know, by any chance,
What rose-leaf ashes of romance
Are faintly stirred by later days
That would be well enough, she says,
If only people were more wise,
And grown-up children used their eyes.

THE MILL

The miller's wife had waited long,
   The tea was cold, the fire was dead;
And there might yet be nothing wrong
   In how he went and what he said:
'There are no millers any more.'
   Was all that she had heard him say;
And he had lingered at the door
   So long that it seemed yesterday.

Sick with a fear that had no form
   She knew that she was there at last;
And in the mill there was a warm
   And mealy fragrance of the past.
What else there was would only seem
   To say again what he had meant;
And what was hanging from a beam
   Would not have heeded where she went.

And if she thought it followed her,
   She may have reasoned in the dark
That one way of the few there were
   Would hide her and would leave no mark:
Black water, smooth above the weir
   Like starry velvet in the night,
Though ruffled once, would soon appear
   The same as ever to the sight.

VAIN GRATUITIES

Never was there a man much uglier
In eyes of other women, or more grim:
'The Lord has filled her chalice to the brim,
So let us pray she's a philosopher,'
They said; and there was more they said of her –
Deeming it, after twenty years with him,
No wonder that she kept her figure slim
And always made you think of lavender.

But she, demure as ever, and as fair,
Almost, as they remembered her before
She found him, would have laughed had she been there;
And all they said would have been heard no more
Than foam that washes on an island shore
Where there are none to listen or to care.

THE UNFORGIVEN

When he, who is the unforgiven,
Beheld her first, he found her fair:
No promise ever dreamt in heaven
Could then have lured him anywhere
That would have been away from there;
And all his wits had lightly striven,
Foiled with her voice, and eyes, and hair.

There's nothing in the saints and sages
To meet the shafts her glances had,
Or such as hers have had for ages
To blind a man till he be glad,
And humble him till he be mad.
The story would have many pages,
And would be neither good nor bad.

And, having followed, you would find him
Where properly the play begins;
But look for no red light behind him –
No fumes of many-coloured sins,
Fanned high by screaming violins.
God knows what good it was to blind him,
Or whether man or woman wins.

And by the same eternal token,
Who knows how just it will all end? –
This drama of hard words unspoken,

This fireside farce, without a friend
Or enemy to comprehend
What augurs when two lives are broken,
And fear finds nothing left to mend.

He stares in vain for what awaits him,
And sees in Love a coin to toss;
He smiles, and her cold hush berates him
Beneath his hard half of the cross;
They wonder why it ever was;
And she, the unforgiving, hates him
More for her lack than for her loss.

He feeds with pride his indecision,
And shrinks from what will not occur,
Bequeathing with infirm derision
His ashes to the days that were,
Before she made him prisoner;
And labors to retrieve the vision
That he must once have had of her.

He waits, and there awaits an ending,
And he knows neither what nor when;
But no magicians are attending
To make him see as he saw then,
And he will never find again
The face that once had been the rending
Of all his purpose among men.

He blames her not, nor does he chide her,
And she has nothing new to say;
If he were Bluebeard he could hide her,
But that's not written in the play,
And there will be no change to-day;
Although, to the serene outsider,
There still would seem to be a way.

BEWICK FINZER

Time was when his half million drew
    The breath of six per cent;
But soon the worm of what-was-not
    Fed hard on his content;
And something crumbled in his brain
    When his half million went.

Time passed, and filled along with his
    The place of many more;
Time came, and hardly one of us
    Had credence to restore,
From what appeared one day, the man
    Whom we had known before.

The broken voice, the withered neck,
    The coat worn out with care,
The cleanliness of indigence,
    The brilliance of despair,
The fond imponderable dreams
    Of affluence, – all were there.

Poor Finzer, with his dreams and schemes,
    Fares hard now in the race,
With heart and eye that have a task
    When he looks in the face
Of one who might so easily
    Have been in Finzer's place.

He comes unfailing for the loan
    We give and then forget;
He comes, and probably for years
    Will he be coming yet, –
Familiar as an old mistake,
    And futile as regret.

RICHARD CORY

Whenever Richard Cory went down town,
We people on the pavement looked at him:
He was a gentleman from sole to crown,
Clean favored, and imperially slim.

And he was always quietly arrayed,
And he was always human when he talked;
But still he fluttered pulses when he said,
'Good morning,' and he glittered when he walked.

And he was rich – yes, richer than a king –
And admirably schooled in every grace:
In fine, we thought that he was everything
To make us wish that we were in his place.

So on we worked, and waited for the light,
And went without the meat, and cursed the bread;
And Richard Cory, one calm summer night,
Went home and put a bullet through his head.

REUBEN BRIGHT

Because he was a butcher and thereby
Did earn an honest living (and did right),
I would not have you think that Reuben Bright
Was any more a brute than you or I;
For when they told him that his wife must die,
He stared at them, and shook with grief and fright,
And cried like a great baby half the night,
And made the women cry to see him cry.

And after she was dead, and he had paid
The singers and the sexton and the rest,
He packed a lot of things that she had made
Most mournfully away in an old chest
Of hers, and put some chopped-up cedar boughs
In with them, and tore down the slaughter house.

CALVERLY'S

We go no more to Calverly's,
For there the lights are few and low;
And who are there to see by them,
Or what they see, we do not know.
Poor strangers of another tongue
May now creep in from anywhere,
And we, forgotten, be no more
Than twilight on a ruin there.

We two, the remnant. All the rest
Are cold and quiet. You nor I,
Nor fiddle now, nor flagon-lid,
May ring them back from where they lie.
No fame delays oblivion
For them, but something yet survives:
A record written fair, could we
But read the book of scattered lives.

There'll be a page for Leffingwell,
And one for Lingard, the Moon-calf;
And who knows what for Clavering,
Who died because he couldn't laugh?
Who knows or cares? No sign is here,
No face, no voice, no memory;
No Lingard with his eerie joy,
No Clavering, no Calverly.

We cannot have them here with us
To say where their light lives are gone,
Or if they be of other stuff
Than are the moons of Ilion.
So, be their place of one estate
With ashes, echoes, and old wars, –
Or ever we be of the night,
Or we be lost among the stars.

THE DARK HILLS

Dark hills at evening in the west,
Where sunset hovers like a sound
Of golden horns that sang to rest
Old bones of warriors under ground,
For now from all the bannered ways
Where flash the legions of the sun,
You fade – as if the last of days
Were fading, and all wars were done.

TACT

Observant of the way she told
    So much of what was true,
No vanity could long withhold
    Regard that was her due:
She spared him the familiar guile
    So easily achieved,
That only made a man to smile
    And left him undeceived.

Aware that all imagining
    Of more than what she meant
Would urge an end of everything,
    He stayed; and when he went,
They parted with a merry word
    That was to him as light
As any that was ever heard
    Upon a starry night.

She smiled a little, knowing well
    That he would not remark
The ruins of a day that fell
    Around her in the dark:
He saw no ruins anywhere,
    Nor fancied there were scars
On anyone who lingered there.
    Alone below the stars.

THE TREE IN PAMELA'S GARDEN

Pamela was too gentle to deceive
Her roses. 'Let the men stay where they are,'
She said, 'and if Apollo's avatar
Be one of them, I shall not have to grieve.'
And so she made all Tilbury Town believe
She sighed a little more for the North Star
Than over men, and only in so far
As she was in a garden was like Eve.

Her neighbors – doing all that neighbors can
To make romance of reticence meanwhile –
Seeing that she had never loved a man,
Wished Pamela had a cat, or a small bird,
And only would have wondered at her smile
Could they have seen that she had overheard.

CAPUT MORTUUM

Not even if with a wizard force I might
Have summoned whomsoever I would name,
Should anyone else have come than he who came,
Uncalled, to share with me my fire that night;
For though I should have said that all was right,
Or right enough, nothing had been the same
As when I found him there before the flame,
Always a welcome and a useful sight.

Unfailing and exuberant all the time,
Having no gold he paid with golden rhyme,
Of older coinage than his old defeat,
A debt that like himself was obsolete
In Art's long hazard, where no man may choose
Whether he play to win or toil to lose.

REUNION

By some derision of wild circumstance
Not then our pleasure somehow to perceive,
Last night we fell together to achieve
A light eclipse of years. But the pale chance
Of youth resumed was lost. Time gave a glance
At each of us, and there was no reprieve;
And when there was at last a way to leave,
Farewell was a foreseen extravagance.

Tonight the west has yet a failing red,
While silence whispers of all things not here;
And round there where the fire was that is dead,
Dusk-hidden tenants that are chairs appear.
The same old stars will soon be overhead,
But not so friendly and not quite so near.

STAFFORD'S CABIN

Once there was a cabin here, and once there was a man;
And something happened here before my memory began.
Time has made the two of them the fuel of one flame
And all we have of them is now a legend and a name.

All I have to say is what an old man said to me,
And that would seem to be as much as there will ever be.
'Fifty years ago it was we found it where it sat.' –
And forty years ago it was old Archibald said that

'An apple tree that's yet alive saw something, I suppose,
Of what it was that happened there, and what no mortal knows.
Some one on the mountain heard far off a master shriek,
And then there was a light that showed the way for men to seek.

'We found it in the morning with an iron bar behind,
And there were chains around it; but no search could ever find,
Either in the ashes that were left, or anywhere,
A sign to tell of who or what had been with Stafford there.

'Stafford was a likely man with ideas of his own –
Though I could never like the kind that likes to live alone;
And when you met, you found his eyes were always on your shoes,
As if they did the talking when he asked you for the news.

'That's all my son. Were I to talk for half a hundred years
I'd never clear away from there the cloud that never clears.
We buried what was left of it, – the bar, too, and the chains;
And only for the apple tree there's nothing that remains.'

Forty years ago it was I heard the old man say,
'That's all my son.' – And here again I find the place today,
Deserted and told only by the tree that knows the most,
And overgrown with golden-rod as if there were no ghost.

EXIT

For what we owe to other days,
Before we poisoned him with praise,
May we who shrank to find him weak
Remember that he cannot speak.

For envy that we may recall,
And for our faith before the fall,
May we who are alive be slow
To tell what we shall never know.

For penance he would not confess,
And for the fateful emptiness
Of early triumph undermined,
May we now venture to be kind.

HECTOR KANE

If Hector Kane at eighty-five
Was not the youngest man alive,
Appearance had anointed him
   With undiminished youth.
To look at him was to believe
That as we ask we may receive,
Annoyed by no such evil whim
   As death, or time, or truth.

Which is to doubt, if any of you,
Seeing him, had believed him true.
He was too young to be so old,
   Too old to be so fair.
Beneath a snowy crown of curls,
His cheeks that might have been a girl's
Were certainly, if truth were told,
   Too rose-like to be there.

But Hector was a child of earth,
And would have held of little worth
Reflection or misgiving cast
   On his reality.
It was a melancholy crime.
No less, to torture life with time;
And whoso did was first and last
   Creation's enemy.

He told us, one convivial night,
When younger men were not so bright
Or brisk as he, how he had spared
　　His heart a world of pain,
Merely by seeing always clear
What most it was he wanted here,
And having it when most he cared,
　　And having it again.

'You children of threescore or so,'
He said, 'had best begin to know
If your infirmities that ache,
　　Your lethargies and fears,
And doubts, are mostly more or less
Like things a drunkard in distress
May count with horror, while you shake
　　For counting days and years.

'Nothing was ever true for me
Until I found it so,' said he;
'So time for me has always been
　　Four letters of a word.
Time? Is it anything to eat?
Or maybe it has legs and feet,
To go so as to be unseen;
　　Or maybe it's a bird.

'Years? I have never seen such things.
Why let your fancy give them wings
To lift you from experience
    And carry you astray?
If only you will not be old,
Your mines will give you more than gold,
And for a cheerful diligence
    Will keep the worm away.

'We die of what we eat and drink,
But more we die of what we think;
For which you see me still as young
    At heart as heretofore.
So here's to what's awaiting us –
Cras ingens iterabimus – '
A clutch of wonder gripped his tongue,
    And Hector said no more.

Serene and inarticulate
He lay, for us to contemplate.
The mortal trick, we all agreed,
    Was never better turned:
Bequeathing us to time and care,
He told us yet that we were there
To make as much as we could read
    Of all that he had learned.

JOHN GORHAM

'Tell me what you're doing over here, John Gorham,
Sighing hard and seeming to be sorry when you're not;
Make me laugh or let me go now, for long faces in the moonlight
Are a sign for me to say again a word that you forgot.' –

'I'm over here to tell you what the moon already
May have said or maybe shouted ever since a year ago;
I'm over here to tell you what you are, Jane Wayland,
And to make you rather sorry, I should say, for being so.' –

'Tell me what you're saying to me now, John Gorham,
Or you'll never see as much of me as ribbons any more,
I'll vanish in as many ways as I have toes and fingers,
And you'll not follow far for one where flocks have been
    before.' –

'I'm sorry now you never saw the flocks, Jane Wayland,
But you're the one to make of them as many as you need.
And then about the vanishing. It's I who mean to vanish;
And when I'm here no longer you'll be done with me indeed.' –

'That's a way to tell me what I am, John Gorham!
How am I to know myself until I make you smile?
Try to look as if the moon were making faces at you,
And a little more as if you meant to stay a little while.' –

'You are what it is that over rose-blown gardens
Makes a pretty flutter for a season in the sun;
You are what it is that with a mouse, Jane Wayland,
Catches him and lets him go and eats him up for fun.' –

'Sure I never took you for a mouse, John Gorham;
All you say is easy; but so far from being true
That I wish you wouldn't ever be again the one to think so;
For it isn't cats and butterflies that I would be to you.' –

'All your little animals are in one picture –
One I've had before me since a year ago tonight;
And the picture where they live will be of you, Jane Wayland,
Till you find a way to kill them or to keep them out of sight.' –

'Won't you ever see me as I am, John Gorham,
Leaving out the foolishness and all I never meant?
Somewhere in me there's a woman, if you know the way
    to find her.
Will you like me any better if I prove it and repent?' –

'I doubt if I shall ever have the time, Jane Wayland,
And I dare say all this moonlight lying round us might as well
Fall for nothing on the shards of broken urns that are forgotten
As on two that have no longer much of anything to tell.'

LEONORA

They have made for Leonora this low dwelling in the ground,
And with cedar they have woven the four walls round.
Like a little dryad hiding she'll be wrapped all in green,
Better kept and longer valued than by ways that would have been.

They will come with many roses in the early afternoon,
They will come with pinks and lilies and with Leonora soon;
And as long as beauty's garments over beauty's limbs are thrown,
There'll be lilies that are liars, and the rose will have its own.

There will be a wondrous quiet in the house that they have made,
And tonight will be a darkness in the place where she'll be laid;
But the builders, looking forward into time, could only see
Darker nights for Leonora than tonight shall ever be.

NEIGHBORS

As often as we thought of her,
  We thought of a gray life
That made a quaint economist
  Of a wolf-hunted wife;
We made the best of all she bore
  That was not ours to bear,
And honored her for wearing things
  That were not things to wear.

There was a distance in her look
  That made us look again;
And if she smiled, we might believe
  That we had looked in vain.
Rarely she came inside our doors,
  And had not long to stay;
And when she left, it seemed somehow
  That she was far away.

At last, when we had all forgot
  That all is here to change,
A shadow on the commonplace
  Was for a moment strange.
Yet there was nothing for surprise,
  Nor much that need be told:
Love, with his gift of pain, had given
  More than one heart could hold.

THE FLYING DUTCHMAN

Unyielding in the pride of his defiance,
    Afloat with none to serve or to command,
Lord of himself at last, and all by Science,
    He seeks the Vanished Land.

Alone, by the one light of his one thought,
    He steers to find the shore from which we came,
Fearless of in what coil he may be caught
    On seas that have no name.

Into the night he sails; and after night
    There is a dawning, though there be no sun;
Wherefore, with nothing but himself in sight,
    Unsighted, he sails on.

At last there is a lifting of the cloud
    Between the flood before him and the sky;
And then – though he may curse the Power aloud
    That has no power to die –

He steers himself away from what is haunted
    By the old ghost of what has been before, –
Abandoning, as always, and undaunted,
    One fog-walled island more.

ARCHIBALD'S EXAMPLE

Old Archibald, in his eternal chair,
Where trespassers, whatever their degree,
Were soon frowned out again, was looking off
Across the clover when he said to me:

'My green hill yonder, where the sun goes down
Without a scratch, was once inhabited
By trees which injured him – and evil trash
That made a cage, and held him while he bled.

'Gone thirty years, I see them as they were
Before they fell. They were a crooked lot
To spoil my sunset, and I saw no time
In fifty years for crooked things to rot.

'Trees, yes; but not a service or a joy
To God or man, for they were thieves of light.
So down they came. Nature and I looked on,
And we were glad when they were out of sight.

'Trees are like men, sometimes; and that being so,
So much for that.' He twinkled in his chair,
And looked across the clover to the place
That he remembered when the trees were there.

FIRELIGHT

Ten years together without yet a cloud,
They seek each other's eyes at intervals
Of gratefulness to firelight and four walls
For love's obliteration of the crowd.
Serenely and perennially endowed
And bowered as few may be, their joy recalls
No snake, no sword, and over them there falls
The blessing of what neither says aloud.

Wiser for silence, they were not so glad
Were she to read the graven tale of lines
On the wan face of one somewhere alone;
Nor were they more content could he have had
Her thoughts a moment since of one who shines
Apart, and would be hers if he had known.

AS IT LOOKED THEN

In a sick shade of spruce, moss-webbed, rock-fed,
Where, long unfollowed by sagacious man,
A scrub that once had been a pathway ran
Blindly from nowhere and to nowhere led,
One might as well have been among the dead
As half way there alive; so I began
Like a malingering pioneer to plan
A vain return – with one last look ahead.

And it was then that like a spoken word
Where there was none to speak, insensibly
A flash of blue that might have been a bird
Grew soon to the calm wonder of the sea –
Calm as a quiet sky that looked to be
Arching a world where nothing had occurred.

A CHRISTMAS SONNET
For One in Doubt

While you that in your sorrow disavow
Service and hope, see love and brotherhood
Far off as ever, it will do no good
For you to wear his thorns upon your brow
For doubt of him. And should you question how
To serve him best, he might say, if he could,
'Whether or not the cross was made of wood
Whereon you nailed me, is no matter now.'

Though other saviors have in older lore
A Legend, and for older gods have died –
Though death may wear the crown it always wore
And ignorance be still the sword of pride –
Something is here that was not here before,
And strangely has not yet been crucified.

FLAMMONDE

The man Flammonde, from God knows where,
With firm address and foreign air,
With news of nations in his talk
And something royal in his walk,
With glint of iron in his eyes,
But never doubt, nor yet surprise,
Appeared, and stayed, and held his head
As one by kings accredited.

Erect, with his alert repose
About him, and about his clothes,
He pictured all tradition hears
Of what we owe to fifty years.
His cleansing heritage of taste
Paraded neither want nor waste;
And what he needed for his fee
To live, he borrowed graciously.

He never told us what he was,
Or what mischance, or other cause,
Had banished him from better days
To play the Prince of Castaways.
Meanwhile he played surpassing well
A part, for most, unplayable;
In fine, one pauses, half afraid
To say for certain that he played.

For that, one may as well forego
Conviction as to yes or no;
Nor can I say just how intense
Would then have been the difference
To several, who, having striven
In vain to get what he was given,
Would see the stranger taken on
By friends not easy to be won.

Moreover, many a malcontent
He soothed and found munificent;
His courtesy beguiled and foiled
Suspicion that his years were soiled;
His mien distinguished any crowd,
His credit strengthened when he bowed;
And women, young and old, were fond
Of looking at the man Flammonde.

There was a woman in our town
Of whom the fashion was to frown;
But while our talk renewed the tinge
Of a long-faded scarlet fringe,
The man Flammonde saw none of that,
And what he saw we wondered at –
That none of us, in her distress,
Could hide or find our littleness.

There was a boy that all agreed
Had shut within him the rare seed
Of learning. We could understand,
But none of us could lift a hand.
The man Flammonde appraised the youth,
And told a few of us the truth;
And thereby, for a little gold,
A flowered future was unrolled.

There were two citizens who fought
For years and years, and over nought;
They made life awkward for their friends,
And shortened their own dividends.
The man Flammonde said what was wrong
Should be made right; nor was it long
Before they were again in line,
And had each other in to dine.

And these I mention are but four
Of many out of many more.
So much for them. But what of him –
So firm in every look and limb?
What small satanic sort of kink
Was in his brain? What broken link
Withheld him from the destinies
That came so near to being his?

What was he, when we came to sift
His meaning, and to note the drift
Of incommunicable ways
That make us ponder while we praise?
Why was it that his charm revealed
Somehow the surface of a shield?
What was it that we never caught?
What was he, and what was he not?

How much it was of him we met
We cannot ever know; nor yet
Shall all he gave us quite atone
For what was his, and his alone;
Nor need we now, since he knew best,
Nourish an ethical unrest:
Rarely at once will nature give
The power to be Flammonde and live.

We cannot know how much we learn
From those who never will return,
Until a flash of unforeseen
Remembrance falls on what has been.
We've each a darkening hill to climb;
And this is why, from time to time
In Tilbury Town, we look beyond
Horizons for the man Flammonde.

AN OLD STORY

Strange that I did not know him then,
    That friend of mine!
I did not even show him then
    One friendly sign;

But cursed him for the ways he had
    To make me see
My envy of the praise he had
    For praising me.

I would have rid the earth of him
    Once, in my pride ...
I never knew the worth of him
    Until he died.

BALLADE OF THE BROKEN FLUTES

To A.T. Schumann

In dreams I crossed a barren land,
   A land of ruin, far away;
Around me hung on every hand
   A deathful stillness of decay;
   And silent, as in bleak dismay
That song should thus foresaken be,
   On that forgotten ground there lay
The broken flutes of Arcady.

The forest that was all so grand
   When pipes and tabors had their sway
Stood leafless now, a ghostly band
   Of skeletons in cold array.
   A lonely surge of ancient spray
Told of an unforgetful sea,
   But iron blows had hushed for aye
The broken flutes of Arcady.

No more by summer breezes fanned,
   The place was desolate and gray;
But still my dream was to command
   New life into that shrunken clay.
   I tried it. And you scan today,
With uncommiserating glee,
   The songs of one who strove to play
The broken flutes of Arcady.

So, Rock, I join the common fray,
　　To fight where Mammon may decree;
And leave, to crumble as they may,
　　The broken flutes of Arcady.

THE DEAD VILLAGE

Here there is death. But even here, they say,
Here where the dull sun shines this afternoon
As desolate as ever the dead moon
Did glimmer on dead Sardis, men were gay;
And there were little children here to play,
With small soft hands that once did keep in tune
The strings that stretch from heaven, till too soon
The change came, and the music passed away.

Now there is nothing but the ghost of things –
No life, no love, no children, and no men;
And over the forgotten place there clings
The strange and unrememberable light
That is in dreams. The music failed, and then
God frowned, and shut the village from His sight.

THE RETURN OF MORGAN AND FINGAL

And there we were together again –
　　Together again, we three:
Morgan, Fingal, fiddle, and all,
　　They had come for the night with me.

The spirit of joy was in Morgan's wrist,
　　There were songs in Fingal's throat;
And secure outside, for the spray to drench,
　　Was a tossed and empty boat.

And there were the pipes, and there was the punch,
　　And somewhere were twelve years;
So it came, in the manner of things unsought,
　　That a quick knock vexed our ears.

The night wind hovered and shrieked and snarled,
　　And I heard Fingal swear;
Then I opened the door – but I found no more
　　Than a chalk-skinned woman there.

I looked, and at last, 'What is it?' I said –
　　'What is it that we can do?'
But never a word could I get from her
　　But 'You – you three – it is you!'

Now the sense of a crazy speech like that
    Was more than a man could make;
So I said, 'But we – we are what, we three?'
    And I saw the creature shake.

'Be quick!' she cried, 'for I left her dead –
    And I was afraid to come;
But you, you three – God made it be –
    Will ferry the dead girl home.

'Be quick! Be quick! – but listen to that
    Who is that makes it? – hark!'
But I heard no more than a knocking splash
    And a wind that shook the dark.

'It is only the wind that blows,' I said,
    'And the boat that rocks outside.'
And I watched her there, and pitied her there –
    'Be quick! Be quick!' she cried.

She cried so loud that her voice went in
    To find where my two friends were;
So Morgan came, and Fingal came,
    And out we went with her.

'Twas a lonely way for a man to take
    And a fearsome way for three;
And over the water, and all day long,
    They had come for the night with me.

But the girl was dead, as the woman had said,
    And the best we could see to do
Was to lay her aboard. The north wind roared,
    And into the night we flew.

Four of us living and one for a ghost
    Furrowing crest and swell,
Through the surge and the dark, for that faint far spark,
    We ploughed with Azrael.

Three of us ruffled and one gone mad,
    Crashing to south we went;
And three of us there were too spattered to care
    What this late sailing meant.

So down we steered and along we tore
    Through the flash of the midnight foam:
Silent enough to be ghosts on guard
    We ferried the dead girl home.

We ferried her down to the voiceless wharf,
    And we carried her up to the light;
And we left the two to the father there,
    Who counted the coals that night.

Then back we steered through the foam again,
    But our thoughts were fast and few;
And all we did was to crowd the surge
    And to measure the life we knew; –

Till at last we came where a dancing gleam
    Skipped out to us, we three, –
And the dark wet mooring pointed home
    Like a finger from the sea.

Then out we pushed the teetering skiff
    And in we drew to the stairs;
And up we went, each man content
    With a life that fed no cares.

Fingers were cold and feet were cold,
    And the tide was cold and rough;
But the light was warm, and the room was warm,
    And the world was good enough.

And there were the pipes, and there was the punch,
    More shrewd than Satan's tears:
Fingal had fashioned it, all by himself,
    With a craft that comes of years.

And there we were together again –
    Together again, we three:
Morgan, Fingal, fiddle, and all,
    They were there for the night with me.

ALMA MATER

He knocked, and I beheld him at the door –
A vision for the gods to verify.
'What battered ancientry is this,' thought I,
'And when, if ever, did we meet before?'
But ask him as I might, I got no more
For answer than a moaning and a cry:
Too late to parley, but in time to die,
He staggered, and lay shapeless on the floor.

When had I known him? And what brought him here?
Love, warning, malediction, hunger, fear?
Surely I never thwarted such as he? –
Again, what soiled obscurity was this:
Out of what scum, and up from what abyss,
Had they arrived – these rags of memory?

CLAVERING

I say no more for Clavering
    Than I should say of him who fails
To bring his wounded vessel home
    When reft of rudder and of sails;

I say no more than I should say
    Of any other one who sees
Too far for guidance of today,
    Too near for the eternities.

I think of him as I should think
    Of one who for scant wages played,
And faintly, a flawed instrument
    That fell while it was being made;

I think of him as one who fared,
    Unfaltering and undeceived,
Amid mirages of renown
    And urgings of the unachieved;

I think of him as one who gave
    To Lingard leave to be amused,
And listened with a patient grace
    That we, the wise ones, had refused;

I think of metres that he wrote
    For Cubit, the ophidian guest:
'What Lilith, or Dark Lady' ... Well.
    Time swallows Cubit with the rest.

I think of last words that he said
    One midnight over Calverly:
'Good-by – good man.' He was not good;
    So Clavering was wrong, you see.

I wonder what has come to pass
    Could he have borrowed for a spell
The fiery-frantic indolence
    That made a ghost of Leffingwell;

I wonder if he pitied us
    Who cautioned him till he was gray
To build his house with ours on earth
    And have an end of yesterday;

I wonder what it was we saw
    To make us think that we were strong;
I wonder if he saw too much,
    Or if he looked one way too long.

But when were thoughts or wonderings
    To ferret out the man within?
Why prate of what he seemed to be,
    And all that he might not have been?

He clung to phantoms and to friends,
   And never came to anything.
He left a wreath on Cubit's grave.
   I say no more for Clavering.

THE COMPANION

Let him answer as he will,
Or be lightsome as he may,
Now nor after shall he say
Worn-out words enough to kill,
Or to lull down by their craft,
Doubt, that was born yesterday,
When he lied and when she laughed.

Let him find another name
For the starlight on the snow,
Let him teach her till she know
That all seasons are the same,
And all sheltered ways are fair, –
Still, wherever she may go,
Doubt will have a dwelling there.

THE FALSE GODS

'We are false and evanescent, and aware of our deceit,
From the straw that is our vitals to the clay that is our feet.
You may serve us if you must, and you shall have your wage of
    ashes, –
Though arrears due thereafter may be hard for you to meet.

'You may swear that we are solid, you may say that we are strong,
But we know that we are neither and we say that you are wrong;
You may find an easy worship in acclaiming our indulgence,
But your large admiration of us now is not for long.

'If your doom is to adore us with a doubt that's never still,
And you pray to see our faces – pray in earnest, and you will.
You may gaze at us and live, and live assured of our confusion:
For the False Gods are mortal, and are made for you to kill.

'And you may as well observe, while apprehensively at ease
With an Art that's inorganic and is anything you please,
That anon your newest ruin may lie crumbling unregarded,
Like an old shrine forgotten in a forest of new trees.

'Howsoever like no other be the mode you may employ,
There's an order in the ages for the ages to enjoy;
Though the temples you are shaping and the passions you are
    singing
Are a long way from Athens and a longer way from Troy.

'When we promise more than ever of what never shall arrive,
And you seem a little more than ordinarily alive,
Make a note that you are sure you understand our obligations –
For there's grief always abiding where two and two are five.

'There was this for us to say and there was this for you to know,
Though it humbles and it hurts us when we have to tell you so
If you doubt the only truth in all our perjured composition,
May the True Gods attend you and forget us when we go.'

THE RAT

As often as he let himself be seen
We pitied him, or scorned him, or deplored
The inscrutable profusion of the Lord
Who shaped as one of us a thing so mean –
Who made him human when he might have been
A rat, and so been wholly in accord
With any other creature we abhorred
As always useless and not always clean.

Now he is hiding all alone somewhere,
And in a final hole not ready then;
For now he is among those over there
Who are not coming back to us again.
And we who do the fiction of our share
Say less of rats and rather more of men.

THE SHEAVES

Where long the shadows of the wind had rolled,
Green wheat was yielding to the change assigned;
And as by some vast magic undivined
The world was turning slowly into gold.
Like nothing that was ever bought or sold
It waited there, the body and the mind;
And with a mighty meaning of a kind
That tells the more the more it is not told.

So in a land where all days are not fair,
Fair days went on till on another day
A thousand golden sheaves were lying there,
Shining and still, but not for long to stay –
As if a thousand girls with golden hair
Might rise from where they slept and go away.

WHY HE WAS THERE

Much as he left it when he went from us
Here was the room again where he had been
So long that something of him should be seen,
Or felt – and so it was. Incredulous,
I turned about, loath to be greeted thus,
And there he was in his old chair, serene
As ever, and as laconic and as lean
As when he lived, and as cadaverous.

Calm as he was of old when we were young,
He sat there gazing at the pallid flame
Before him. 'And how far will this go on?'
I thought. He felt the failure of my tongue,
And smiled: 'I was not here until you came;
And I shall not be here when you are gone.'

THE WOMAN AND THE WIFE

1. The Explanation

'You thought we knew,' she said, 'but we were wrong.
This we can say, the rest we do not say;
Nor do I let you throw yourself away
Because you love me. Let us both be strong,
And we shall find in sorrow, before long,
Only the price Love ruled that we should pay:
The dark is at the end of every day,
And silence is the end of every song.

'You ask me for one proof that I speak right,
But I can answer only what I know;
You look for just one lie to make black white,
But I can tell you only what is true –
God never made me for the wife of you.
This we can say, – believe me! ... Tell me so!'

2. The Anniversary

'Give me the truth, whatever it may be.
You thought we knew, now tell me what you miss:
You are the one to tell me what it is –
You are a man, and you have married me.
What is it worth tonight that you can see
More marriage in the dream of one dead kiss

Than in a thousand years of life like this?
Passion has turned the lock, Pride keeps the key.

'Whatever I have said or left unsaid,
Whatever I have done or left undone, –
Tell me. Tell me the truth ... Are you afraid?
Do you think that Love was ever fed with lies
But hunger lived thereafter in his eyes?
Do you ask me to take moonlight for the sun?'

ANOTHER DARK LADY

Think not, because I wonder where you fled,
That I would lift a pin to see you there;
You may, for me, be prowling anywhere,
So long as you show not your little head:
No dark and evil story of the dead
Would leave you less pernicious or less fair –
Not even Lilith, with her famous hair;
And Lilith was the devil, I have read.

I cannot hate you, for I loved you then.
The woods were golden then. There was a road
Through beeches; and I said their smooth feet showed
Like yours. Truth must have heard me from afar,
For I shall never have to learn again
That yours are cloven as no beech's are.

DEMOS

1.

All you that are enamored of my name
   And less intent on what most I require,
   Beware, for my design and your desire,
Deplorably, are not as yet the same.
Beware, I say, the failure and the shame
   Of losing that for which you now aspire
   So blindly, and of hazarding entire
The gift that I was bringing when I came.

Give as I will, I cannot give you sight
   Whereby to see that with you there are some
   To lead you, and be led. But they are dumb
Before the wrangling and the shrill delight
   Of your deliverance that has not come,
And shall not, if I fail you – as I might.

2.

So little have you seen of what awaits
   Your fevered glimpse of a democracy
   Confused and foiled with an equality
Not equal to the envy it creates,
That you see not how near you are the gates
   Of an old king who listens fearfully
   To you that are outside and are to be
The noisy lords of imminent estates.

Rather be then your prayer that you shall have
    Your kingdom undishonored. Having all,
    See not the great among you for the small,
But hear their silence; for the few shall save
    The many, or the many are to fall –
Still to be wrangling in a noisy grave.

LOST ANCHORS

Like a dry fish flung inland far from shore,
There lived a sailor, warped and ocean-browned,
Who told of an old vessel, harbor-drowned
And out of mind a century before,
Where divers, on descending to explore
A legend that had lived its way around
The world of ships, in the dark hulk had found
Anchors, which had been seized and seen no more.

Improving a dry leisure to invest
Their misadventure with a manifest
Analogy that he may read who runs,
The sailor made it old as ocean grass –
Telling of much that once had come to pass
With him, whose mother should have had no sons.

A SHORT BIBLIOGRAPHY

POETRY COLLECTIONS/SELECTIONS PRIOR TO 2000

Selected Poems (ed Robert Faggen) Penguin Twentieth Century Classics, 1997

The Essential Robinson (ed Donald Hall) The Ecco Press, 1994

The Poetry of E.A. Robinson (ed Robert Mezey) The Modern Library, New York, 1999

POETRY COLLECTIONS/SELECTIONS SINCE 2000

Edward Arlington Robinson: Poems (selected and edited by Scott Donaldson) New York, Alfred A. Knopf/Everyman Library, 2007

BIOGRAPHY PRIOR TO 2000

Hagedorn, Hermann *Edwin Arlington Robinson*, Macmillan, New York, 1938

BIOGRAPHY SINCE 2000

Donaldson, Scott *Edwin Arlington Robinson: A Poet's Life*, New York, Columbia University Press, 2007 (This has become the definitive biography.)

Grinstein, Alexander and Grinstein, Adele B. *Edwin Arlington Robinson: Child of Scorn*, New York, Universe, 2007

CRITICAL STUDIES PRIOR TO 2000

Coxe, Louis O. *Edwin Arlington Robinson: The Life of Poetry*, Pegasus, New York, 1969

Winters, Yvor *Edwin Arlington Robinson*, New Directions, New York, 1971

Edwin Arlington Robinson: A Collection of Critical Essays (edited by Francis Murphy) Prentice Hall, New Jersey, 1970

SEE ALSO:

Donald E. Stanford's chapter on Robinson in *Revolution and Convention in Modern Poetry*, Associated University Presses, New Jersey, 1983

William H. Pritchard's chapter on Robinson in *Lives of the Modern Poets*, Oxford Univeristy Press, 1980/Faber and Faber, 1980

CRITICAL STUDIES SINCE 2000

Gale, Robert L. *An Edwin Arlington Robinson Encyclopedia*, Jefferson, North Carolina, McFarland, 2006